Mystic Fire

Rosicrucian Writings of A. E. Waite

Edited by Michael R. Poll

Mystic Fire
Rosicrucian Writings of A.E. Waite

A Cornerstone Book
Published by Cornerstone Book Publishers
Copyright © 2008 by Cornerstone Book Publishers

Cornerstone Book Publishers
New Orleans, LA

First Cornerstone Edition - 2008

www.cornerstonepublishers.com

ISBN: 1-934935-09-3
ISBN 13: 978-1-934935-09-5

MADE IN THE USA

Table of Contents

Mystic Fire

A French Method of Fortune-Telling by Cards

THE methods of divination by cards are sufficiently numerous in France, as they are in other countries, including England. Our own, however, are chiefly of continental origin, while, so far as it is possible to speak with any positive opinion upon so dubious and involved a question, it would appear that the French systems are largely particular to themselves, subject of course to the fact that proceeding in all cases on certain general principles, to that extent they may be said to derive from one another, or at least from a common root. I have selected for inclusion one system which- although it first came into notice at the beginning of the nineteenth century is likely to be new to my readers. It is worked with a piquet set of ordinary playing cards, which, as most people will know, consists of the usual picture-pieces and the ace, 10, 9, 8 and 7 of each suit, excluding the lower numbers. The method has appeared, I believe, under more than one auspice, but the imputed author termed himself an Egyptian and claimed to publish his little treatise at Memphis, which, however, stands for Paris. It is not a very full method and is not free from confusions as it was first issued. In the form which here follows it has been so far rectified and extended from other French sources that it will, I think, serve the purpose as an alternative to the English system given in the previous section. I must explain, however, that those who intend to make use of it should obtain, if possible, a set of French or Swiss cards, in which the picture-pieces appear at full length, instead of with a head at either end, and all the numbers are marked Droit and Renverse at their opposing poles, meaning right side up and reversed.

Otherwise, an English set may be so marked by the student. Important differences attach to the variations in question, so far as the trump-cards are concerned, as they do indeed in the English method.

It may not be impertinent to mention before proceeding that the origin of card-playing has been referred by some French writers to one Jacquemin Gringonneur, from whom two sets were purchased in 1392 to amuse Charles VI, King of France, during his days of distraction. It is at most obvious that the simple historical fact can be only an episode in the French history of cards; the evidence is concerning sale and purchase, and it would be fantasy to assume that the vendor in the specific instance was also the inventing artist. Spain and Italy are sometimes said to have been in possession of cards prior to the French people; it has been even speculated that they were brought to Italy by Greek emigrants from Constantinople, that they drifted from Italy into Spain and thence to our Gallic neighbors. It is certain, in any case, that they were in Italy at the very time when their existence is first on record in France, for they are mentioned in a Florentine chronicle written towards the close of the fourteenth century, while so early as 1332 it is said that they were prohibited in Spain by an edict of Alphonsus XI. If the latter statement rests on authority, it leaves the reason doubtful, and I mention this point to add that we have little opportunity of deciding when cards were first used as a game of hazard; it has been thought that at their inception they were designed for instruction or amusement, and contained no combinations of numbers, so essential for gambling arts. The earliest records which I have cited offer no indication of the cards that composed the sets, either as to design or quantity; therefore the symbols and numbers may or may not have corresponded when first we hear concerning them to the Tarot packs, which – either independently or otherwise – were certainly in existence about the same period. It is indubitable, as I have stated already, that these were the precursors of our playing cards, but there are wide differences in most of the archaic sets. It can only be said that the scheme of symbolism which is comprised in the major trumps is unquestionably old, as it is indubitably of great importance, though nearly all that has been written heretofore upon the subject is referable to the realms of reverie. A separate section is devoted, however, to the Tarot elements, the higher construction of their meaning and its application in an exalted sense. It remains only to say that French cartomancy in the eighteenth and nineteenth centuries set the fashion to the whole English-speaking world, if not to Europe itself – that Alliette, or Etteilla, Mlle. Lenormand, Madame Clement and Julia Orsini were the prophets of all divination with all varieties of cards and that, except in certain secret circles, where there is supposed to be a special tradition, we have done little more than follow them.

I will give, in the first place, the general signification of piquet cards according to various authorities, and these may be compared with the alternative renderings which have been enumerated already in connection with the shorter English method. It will be understood, as in other cases, that everything depends upon the insight, intuition, divining gift, or – as it is called somewhat conventionally – the clairvoyant faculty of the operator.

A. - DIAMONDS

The Ace. - Letters, or news at hand otherwise.

King. - Friendship ; if followed by the Queen, marriage; if reversed, impediments, difficulties and the vexations thereto belonging.

Queen. - A woman from the country, who is fair but evil-speaking; reversed, more directly inimical to the Querent in word and also in deed.

Knave. - A postman, valet, postillion, soldier, or messenger bearing news. The news are good if the card is right side up and bad if it appears reversed.

Ten. - Great joy, change of place, a party from the country.

Nine. - Delay and postponement, but not resulting in failure.

Eight. - A man of business or young merchant, who is commercially related to the Querent.

Seven. - Good news, above all if accompanied by the Ace.

B. - HEARTS

The Ace. - Joy, contentment, and-if it is accompanied by several picture-cards - marriages, feasts, etc;, in pleasant company.

King. - A rich man, banker, or financier, well disposed, and may promote the interests of the Querent. If reversed, the person is miserly and to deal with him will prove difficult.

Queen. - An honest, frank and obliging woman; if reversed, there will be some obstacle to a projected marriage.

Knave. - A soldier or young man, who is anxious to promote the Querent's welfare, will play some part in his life and will be allied with him after one or another manner.

Ten. - A surprise, but often one of a kind which will be advantageous as well as agreeable to the consulting party.

Nine. - Concord.

Eight. - Domestic and private happiness, attended by success in undertakings; exceedingly felicitous for the destinies of the middle path, the amenities of the quiet life.

Seven. - Marriage, if the Querent is a lady, and the issue will be daughters only; if a man, it is destined that he will make a rich and happy marriage.

C. - SPADES

The Ace. - In company with the ten and nine, this card signifies death, grief, more especially from bereavement, but also sorrow from many sources; it includes further the idea of treason and possibly of loss by theft or robbery.

King. - A magistrate or lawyer, whose intervention may prove disagreeable; the card reversed signifies loss in a lawsuit or general derangement of affairs.

Queen. - A disappointed woman – possibly a widow in dejection; if reversed, one who is anxious to remarry, unknown to or in spite of her family.

Knave. - Some kind of disgrace which will be inimical to be peace of mind and perhaps even the liberty of the Querent; reversed, serious complications for the person concerned; also betrayal in love, if the Querent is a woman.

Ten. - Imprisonment for a man, if followed by the Ace and King of the same suit; for a woman, disease, illness.

Nine. - Protraction and difficulties in business; followed by the Nine of Diamonds and the Ace of Clubs, delay in the receipt of expected money.

Eight.- Arrival of a person who will carry bad news if followed by the Seven of Diamonds and near to a picture card – whether King, Queen or Knave – tears, discord, destitution or loss of employment.

Seven. - Quarrels, inquietude; if ameliorated by the vicinity of some Hearts, it promises safety, independence and moral consolation.

D. - CLUBS

Ace. - Advantages, commercial and industrial benefits of every kind, easy collection of dues, unmixed prosperity – but these more especially when followed by the Seven of Diamonds and the Seven of Clubs.

King. - An influential, powerful person, who is equitable and benevolent towards the Querent, to whom he will render signal services; but reversed, this personage will experience some difficulty in his proceedings and may be even in danger of failure.

Queen. - A dark woman, rivalry, competitive spirit; in the neighborhood of a card which stands for a man, she will have preference for the man in question; on the contrary, in proximity to a feminine card, she will be in sympathy with the Querent; reversed, she is very covetous, jealous and disposed to infidelity.

Knave. - One who is in love, a proper young man, who pays court to a young lady; placed next to a feminine card, his chances of success are very good; side by side with a man, there is reason to hope that the latter will come actively to his assistance and will contribute to his success, unless the said man should be signified by the Knave of Hearts, which presages a dangerous rivalry; reversed, there is reason to fear opposition to marriage on the part of the person's parents.

Ten. - Prosperity and good fortune of every kind; at the same time, if followed by the Nine of Diamonds a delay is foreshadowed in the return of money; contrary to all, if this card is side by side with the Nine of Spades – which everywhere signifies disappointment – complete failure is promised; so also if the question at stake is a lawsuit, loss is probable.

Nine. - Success in love; for a bachelor or spinster, approaching marriage; for a widow, her second nuptials.

Eight. - A favorable conclusion which may be anticipated by the Querent in financial and business matters.

Seven. - Anxieties occasioned by love-intrigues; followed by the Seven of Diamonds and the Nine of Spades, abundance of good things and rich family inheritances.

MODE OF OPERATION IN SPECIFIED CASES
I
For a Marriage and Similar Subjects

Shuffle the cards of a piquet set and cut three times. If an actual marriage is in question, remove two cards, representing the lover and the lady whose fortunes are at issue. Place these cards, face upwards, on the table before you. As usual, fair people are represented by Hearts and Diamonds but those of dark complexion by Clubs and Spades. The attribution, between these lines, seems to be usually at predilection or discretion, but Diamonds are sometimes taken to signify very fair people and blondes, while Spades are for actual brunettes and very dusky complexions.

Lay out the rest of the cards three by three; in every triplicity which produces two of the same suit, select the higher card of that suit and place it by the side of the other card which stands for the Querent. Throw out the rest for the moment, but they will be required later. When any triplicity produces entirely different suits, put aside all three in the rejected pile. When the entire cards of the set have thus been dealt with in succession, take up the rejected lot, and after shuffling and cutting as before, proceed in the same manner until you have drawn fifteen cards and placed them by the side of the Querent.

If the Querent is a dark man, he will not have his wish regarding the marriage contemplated unless a tierce to the King in Clubs be among the fifteen cards. It may of course happen that the King has been drawn to represent him. If, however; he be a Spade, then alternatively there must be a tierce in Spades.

The same rule obtains if the Querent is a dark young lady, but in addition to a tierce in the suit there must be the Ace of the suit also.

If the Querent is a fair man or woman, then a tierce in the one case and a tierce and the Ace in the other must be found in Hearts or Diamonds according to the grade of their fairness.

If the question concerns a marriage to take place in the country, it has been held by the expositors of the system that a tierce to the King in Diamonds is indispensable. This seems to involve the system in respect of fair people, but it is only a confusion of expression. If Diamonds correspond to the Querent, that tierce must obviously be present, or *ex hypothesi* there will be no marriage; but if present the inference is that the Querent will get his wish in respect of locality as well as of the fact of marriage. On the other hand, if the Querent is referable to any other of the three remaining suits, then *ex hypothesi*, to attain his presumed wish for a country wedding, he must have the tierce in Diamonds as well as in his own suit. It is not very probable that the alternative between town and country will arise as a subsidiary question, and if it does, it might be better to determine it separately by the help of some other system.

It serves no purpose to ignore the shades of complexion in fair people and represent them indifferently by Diamonds, as this would be forcing the oracles and would make the reading void.

Finally, if the marriage question concerns a widower or widow, it is equally essential that the cards drawn should furnish a tierce to the King in Spades and the Ace of Hearts – which again is very hard upon all persons who are not represented by Spades. The inference is that second marriages are rare.

II
For Questions of Inheritance

Shuffle and cut as before, and place on the table a card which is held to typify the Querent. The presence of the Ace of Spades, manifesting right side up, indicates profit in consequence of a death- that is to say, an inheritance or legacy. If the Ace is accompanied by the Seven, Eight, Nine and Ten of Clubs, there will be a large increment of money. The combination may be difficult to secure, but very large inheritances are rarer than second marriages.

III
For Lawsuits and Similar Matters

No judgement can be given on the chances of a lawsuit, actual or pending, nor generally on things of this nature, unless the King of Spades comes out in the dealing. If that card is held usually to represent the Querent, then it only follows automatically that a judgment is possible, and it is so much the easier for him in such case. The shuffling, cutting and dealing proceed as before, and if the Ace in question serves to complete the quint major in Spades- that is, the Ace, King, Queen, Knave and Ten – it is to be feared that the suit will prove good for nothing, either by going against the Querent or bringing him no profit in the opposite case. But if the Ace is accompanied by the four Tens, the chances are excellent. They are said also to be more than good in another event of the dealing which I forbear from dwelling on, as it is practically, if not otherwise, impossible for the fifteen cards- which the dealing proposes to extract- to be all of the red suits. It is well known that compilers of works on cartomancy sometimes forget the limits prescribed by their systems and get consequently into ridiculous plights.

IV
For a Theft

For the discovery of a thief, the presence of the four Knaves is indispensable to any reading, and, as it happens, it is not utterly difficult - though it is none too easy – that the chances of the cards should produce them. The procedure is throughout as before. If the King and the Eight of Spades turn up among the fifteen cards, this means that the thief is already in prison; if the Ace of Spades is among them, the prisoner will be in danger of death; the presence of the Ace of Clubs, the King of Clubs and the Queen of Hearts will afford some hope that the person who stole will himself make restitution; lastly, the predominance of Diamonds offers ground for believing that the thief has been arrested, but on another charge than that which would be preferred by the Querent on his own part.

V

For a Person in Prison

The question at issue is whether the captive has any chance of speedy liberation. The procedure is throughout as before, except that the card selected is held to represent the person in durance instead of the Querent. The fifteen cards having been produced as the result of the working, they should be examined in the usual way. The presence of the Queen of Hearts, Knave of Clubs, Nine of Clubs and the four Aces will give ground for hope that liberation will be easy and at hand. In proportion as these cards are absent, there will be delay in the desired event, and if none are found, it is likely to be rather remote. On the other hand, the appearance of the Eight and Nine of Spades, the King of Spades, and the Knave and Nine of Diamonds, will signify that liberty shall be scarcely obtained, except after many obstacles and much consequent postponement.

VI

For Travellers

It is assumed that the Querent is not himself on a journey but is consulting the oracles for one in whose fortunes he is for some reason interested, by ties of friendship or otherwise. Proceed as before, selecting a card to represent the absent person. When the dealing is finished, the resulting cards should be consulted to ascertain whether they include the Ace of Hearts, the Ace of Diamonds and the Ten of Diamonds, the presence of which will foreshadow probable news. Probability will be raised into certainty by the appearance of the Seven of Diamonds. If, however, the Ten of Spades is found in proximity to the card representing the person who is away on his travels, there will be reason to fear that he is ill; so also the Ace of Spades reversed will mean that he is in other danger than sickness. If he is to succeed in the enterprise that has called him abroad, he will be escorted by the Nine of Hearts, the Ace and the King of Clubs.

Finally, if the Eight of Diamonds is found in relation to his own card, this means that he is on the point of returning.

There is a variation of procedure in all the above cases, which consists in protracting the dealing till twenty-one cards have been drawn instead of fifteen. It is put on record by the so-called Egyptian, speaking from the seat of knowledge, that the predominance of red cards as the result of operation in any given instance foretells great success for the person on whose behalf the consultation is made. The Ace, Ten, Nine, Eight and Seven of Hearts are premonitory of news on which the Querent may be congratulated. The same cards in the suit of Clubs promise success in a lawsuit, or a lucky number in a lottery. The same in the suit of Spades prognosticate news of a relative's death, or that of a friend, but whether there will be profit to the Querent is not so certain, having regard to the generally fatal nature of this suit, the constituents of which may be said almost to constitute the greater misfortunes in cartomancy. The particular numbers in the suit of Diamonds carry with them the same kind of prevision as Hearts.

So far the Egyptian and those who have followed in his footsteps and have extended his method. There are probably several other systems of fortune-telling by means of piquet cards; but as there is no particular authority, so also, and certainly, there is no advantage in thus reducing the elements on which divinatory calculations can be made. The cards below seven in an ordinary pack have their special meanings and therefore their special use. It is obvious that a fuller reading can be obtained with a fuller set, and this is one reason- apart from their incalculably superior symbolism- why Tarot cards, with so many additional numbers, are richer than ordinary cards for the purposes of cartomancy. It should be understood, therefore, that in presenting the French method I am not concerned with recommending it, except in respect of simplicity, to those who are interested in such matters, and although, outside the modes of dealing, I have included from another source only the separate short signification of the two-and-thirty cards, there is no reason why the student or reader should not take advantage of the full pack. Both within and without the present collection, there are ample opportunities to ascertain the significance of the smaller cards; their presence will not stultify the system for those who care to follow it; and, as I have indicated, they help the reading. When the eye of the intuitive mind is open, it is well in things of this kind that the materials on which it can work should not be unreasonably restricted. The thirty-two piquet cards are not the two-and-thirty paths of the absolute according to Kabalism, and so there is no special magic in the lesser number, or if it resides anywhere deeply *perdu*, it has not been given me to find it, a deficiency which I share apparently with those who invented the system, for they have certainly failed to adduce it.

A Journey through the Great Distance

TAKE one more journey with me, just one more journey in dream, looking through the glass of Faerie, which reflects all things. Surely you shall profit because of it, seeing that there are many worlds for winning. The kinds of exchange are many in these visions and curious values attach to them, as you and I might learn in a season of russet apples and golden pippins. There are those who give precious gifts to strangers for a meeting once a year, as you and I shall ensure it, supposing that we are steadfast in dream. There is a Law of Barter in Faerie- as when I sold my birthright in a manger for the price of a star. Once, on another occasion, I was like to have a kingdom in Faerie, but I sold it for manna in the wilderness. Through years that were full, years that were lean, and hollow and empty years I travelled with my pot of manna. I passed through many crowds which knew not whither they went; but I had dreamed of a wild way and was aware of a place which I must reach, through straight and winding paths, going into a great distance. So try one journey more. There is always a white bird flying; it lures and lures and lures; the castles are stranger and stranger; the enchantments deepen and deepen; mystery opens into mystery. I followed this kind of quest, while the moon spelt out the years; but it came to pass, on a day of longing, that I saw low towers of Faerie through the evening mist, in a hushed region of the world. In a mood of contemplation because of them, I sat upon a green knoll which was the place of a wonderful rest. Of what may be said thereon you shall hear when the stars lead you, but of that which may be done after there is no end to the story. When I came to it in that happy hour, the air gave up her who is my Queen in Faerie. Like the heaven which is "about us in our infancy," she shone before me in her purity, bringing the sense of an infinite peace. Hereof is her state in Faerie, and after such manner she intervened, during my life therein. I was haunted by love henceforward, because of this Holy Vision She showed me the jewel which shines at the heart of love, and I held to this great treasure. She taught me saving kisses in Faerie, kisses that break up enchantments, saving kisses that open the world of union. She told me that love in this country is the true, the only talisman; and if you can keep it in your heart, you will never have occasion to enter those halls of painted images, where the "spirit of evil strives for mastery over the spirit of good."

When my Exempt Mistress is seated by her golden harp, you should see how the world goes by- how the world goes by in Faerie and the Crown comes down. It was in offices of music that she came to me more than all- strange music sounding from far away, and pipings of mysterious musicians. The instruments are unearthly in Faerie, and especially among the old hills; but in all that lived and breathed I found that there were lutes and strings in her presence, and I knew at last what is said in quiet places by the wind-harp. There are woes unknown in Faerie and weeping voices in the night-time; but she lifted in sweet music her hands of healing and said unto them: "Peace, be still." She carried the cure by music through wounded reams of Faerie. She opened out all its mysteries in melodious voices. The daisy breathed about her like a choice garden of roses, and the honey-suckle was a sweet incense, as if rising before a high altar. The waterfalls and streams and rivulets ran in light beside her. I saw the rainbow of Faerie shining to the eyes in splendor and beating at the ears in music. The sound of many waters glistened in rainbow colors. The quests of Faerie were set to her subtle melodies, all that wide world over.

She took the thoughts of men upon great voyages. I heard the heart of Faerie throbbing. I heard also such messages in the night-time that my own heart was put to rest.

So did she lead and lead me. As I followed her, faring through the vistas, it was like an echoing far away- beauty and music and grace continued henceforward, stretching into the blue distance. For ever and evermore there were colors and music. The soul was in her eyes of dreaming, and the most dear good God was like another more indrawn music encompassing all her way. I know not what voices they were, but there were some that said "Life of life," and the answer was "Light of Light" – as she passed on her way, when the world rejoiced about her; as she passed slowly through the vistas. Voices and many voices; but I called them Dream-Words of my Mistress. At times the voices and melodies were lifted into a glorious tempest; at others the crash of music- sinking and sinking- dwindled into an utter softness, as of falling petals, as into the silence of a rose-leaf when it rests on a cool sward. In fine, from very far away, came things so high and deep that I know in my own manner some part of the great rest and the great sleep, the living repose of all at the heart of God.

So did she lead and lead me, telling me as we went of the worlds which are beyond Faerie and of the free world of the spirit. Her nimbus was like golden light, seen in the East before morning. We ceased in the end from our foot-farings, all through the great vistas, but we travelled after another manner. There are winged horses in Faerie, and there is a Pegasus which has never yet been put into pound, nor ridden by any poet. It seems to me that I have been looking for him all my life, though I testify that I, speaking these things, have used white wings in my day. I have been where few travellers venture, and I look yet to go further. O the great lands and seas, over which the great people have travelled, and the sea and the land thereafter, of which no one has told! On fair steeds we came out of the world of many images- because of the one image which we had found in our hearts.

We went up a hill in the morning on the other side of Faerie, in a wind of the spirit. And a certain voice fell, which told of the realms beyond. It came about in this manner that even I have beheld with my own eyes, in an hour of clear-seeing, the great end of all travelling.

This is also the end of all stories, like those which I have been telling unto now. Sunset and night-time are over; my Morning-Glory shines in the glory of morning, with gleaming hair

> *"back blown from rosy bands,*
> *And light and joy and fragrance in her hands."*

Hereof is therefore my journey through the great distance, and such is my Swan-Song. I have been making poems of Faerie through my whole life; but this is the end of my poems.

A.E. WAITE.

An Epistle to the Rosicrucian Fraternity

To the most perfectly united, most eminent, most wise, and true philosophers and brothers, R. C., Theodosius Verax, and Theophilus Caelnatus, with health and peace.

WE have no small comfort in beholding those things of which the possession itself would be unlawful. Ambition does oftentimes proceed by impulse where we ourselves would be afraid to go. We seek now to exalt ourselves, supported both by piety and your candor, as it were with wings, above sordid envy and ignorances. Whatsoever judgment ye may form concerning us must be to our profit. If favorable, we shall shortly enjoy an easy boon, but if harsh, the greater our necessities the better will be the opportunity of benevolence. While we are seriously considering that philosophy has been corrupted by the schools, and daily produces more dread monsters than Africa herself, we begin to feel terrified. Aristotle and others of his school have compelled our philosophy to become a mere servant of its own

glory, recognizing no truth but their own inventions. We do not deplore the loss of so many secret writings which having perished in the fire did only at their destruction show signs of brilliancy. Truth is naked, it wears not any mask, and incapable of deceit itself uncovers false persons. Those who pursue truth not only reach the goal but leave a track behind which may be followed by others. For our own part, unless we receive assistance, old age will overtake us, and yet we shall be no further than the threshold. Nevertheless, we prefer to die seeking the goal rather than to yield to shameful idleness. We will accordingly, O most prudent men, continue in earnest desire, looking towards you in whom our help lies! We are sufficiently conscious of our feebleness, and therefore we seek a remedy. The gentle ray of your humanity has animated our sterile hopes and encouraged the vintage song. Where others finished have ye begun. Pardon us, most excellent men, if we speak of those things whereof we are still ignorant! Whatsoever is brought forth into the light under your auspices is deserving of praise. We believe that your book is so much what we need that it might have been written for us alone; we recognize that no ordinary providence has taken us from cimmerian darkness and placed us in a twilight which will shortly be flooded by the rising day. We are not of those conceited Peripatetics who swear by Aristotle, while their books swarm with stupidities. Your philosophy, O most learned men, is not full of kindred absurdities! It displays the greatest secrets in light, and the darkness which blinds most men has sharpened your own eyesight. Furthermore, it is modest and truly learned, and, having fallen from heaven, derives its origin from the Holy Scriptures, wherein nothing is suspicious or erring. Whoever studies these writings will arrive at the knowledge of that matter from which all that lives has been derived. Those who persistently deny that there are men whom God has elected to the knowledge of the intimate mysteries, suspect the solicitude of the Creator, who withholds nothing useful or necessary. He who fabricated the whole machine of the universe for the human race, willed, both for his own glory and our benefit, that His works should be understood. There is, however, no profit in mere study without light from God. Therefore as God, thrice excellent and most great, created the light, wherein all creatures flourish, so a light has kindled over the chaos of letters,
a great cosmos has been produced, heaven has descended to earth, and the superficies being removed the centre itself comes into view,

while if we spoke of even greater things there are some from whom the meaning would not be hidden. For we have good reason to believe that there is a true Society, your own, unto which God has revealed the oracles. It is much more probable that God would reveal such mysteries to his church than to the heathen, and those who possess divine truth are not likely to be ignorant of Nature's secrets. Ye also are few and wise, while the multitude is rude and hurtful, and wise Nature has deeply hidden her treasures that they may not become common. In like manner, art also hath its penetralia; its gems are to be sought, its gold is to be dug up, and the divine operation is an assistant in the investigation of both. Your Fama, translated into the English tongue, has come into our hands, being edited with a preface by the illustrious gentleman E. P. Therein ye have invited worthy persons to join your Society, but hence ye profane! Meanwhile a bitter strife has risen up amongst us, because we are well aware that we deserved not so great a blessing, and yet our weakness gave way before your favor, and we rejoiced at being thus overcome. Another difficulty, notwithstanding, presently appeared, concerning where or to whom we should apply, and we were again plunged into sadness. There was no comfort in the conviction of your wisdom and benevolence if we could not reach you. But in the silence which followed, a sacred voice assured us that the Fraternity we desired so anxiously we should at length find by the grace of God. We have, therefore, cast away fear and again breathe hopefully. Mere gold-seekers have doubtless inquired after you, and so, also, have the votaries of pleasure, whose brains have turned into a belly, while they apply arts to their orgies. But we have followed on the path of Mercury. There are also many given over to much writing, who discourse of the elixir and the panacea in an enigmatic manner, purposing deception, while others coming after them have pretended to find therein what the writers themselves did not know. Let us not be considered thoughtless who have scorned the promises of pseudo-philosophers that we might give ourselves to truth. Those versed in Nature's secrets are taciturn; they do not write much or attractively. Hence little can be gained from books, which are less means of instruction than mental confusion. We therefore ask you to take pity on us; we are still young men and novices, as our nervous epistle indicates, but perhaps an aged mind has been infused into us. As regards religion, we believe in God the Creator and recognize Him in His works. We smile at all which you have said concerning the pope; that religion, if so it can be called, will be involved in the same ruin as other sects and heresies. We trust that there are no other obstacles which separate us from your Society; we ask much, but it is within your power. Pardon us, most loving brethren, if with open arms we seem to force ourselves upon you, and if our desire in itself be pleasing to you, may there be no difficulty from the length of our epistle.

Mysteries of the Holy Graal
in Manifestion and Removal

I - THE INSTITUTION OF THE HALLOWS

IT is a very curious heaven which stands around the infancy of romance-literature, and more than one warrant is required to constitute a full title for the interpretation of the strange signs and portents which are seen in some of its zones. The academies of official learning are consecrated places, and those who have graduated in other schools, and know well that they hold the higher authority, must be the first to recognize and respect the unsleeping vigilance and patience of students who are their colleagues and brothers in a different sphere. In the study of archaic literature, the external history of the texts and the criticism thereto belonging are in the hands of official scholarship, and its authority is usually final; but the inward spirit of the literature is sometimes an essence which escapes the academical process. For example, the implicits of certain books belonging to the cycle of the Holy Graal, as I have endeavoured to express them, would seem to have eluded learning; but any school of criticism which decides that these books do not put forward extraordinary claims of the evasive kind, and do not so far contain the suggestion of an interior meaning, are comparable to those who should say that the effect does not presuppose a cause, and this of necessity. According to those Lesser Histories which I have connected with the name of Robert de Borron, the secret of the Graal, signifying the super-substantial nourishment of man, was communicated by Christ to His chosen disciple Joseph of Arimathaea, who, by preserving the body of the Master after the Crucifixion, became an instrument of the Resurrection. He laid it in the sepulchre, and thus sowed the seed whence issued the archnatural body. On Ascension Day this was removed from the world, but there remained the Holy Vessel, into which the blood of the natural body had been received by Joseph; strangely endued with the virtues of the risen Christ and the power of the Holy Ghost, it sustained him, both spiritually and physically, during forty years of imprisonment; and it was a sign of saving grace, instruction and all wonder to the great company which he led subsequently westward. He committed it in fine to another keeper, by whom it was brought into Britain, and there, or otherwhere, certain lesser hallows were added to the hallow-in-chief, and were held with it in the places of concealment. Those which we meet with more frequently are four in number, but the mystery is really one, since it is all assumed into the Cup. It is understood that for us at least this Cup is a symbol, seeing that the most precious of all vessels are not made with hands. It is in such sense that the true soul of philosophy is a cup which contains the universe. We shall understand also the ministry of material sustenance, sometimes attributed to the Holy Graal, after another manner than can be presumed within the offices of folklore. It is for this reason that the old fable concerning the Bowl of Plenty, as incorporated by the Graal Mystery, assumes a profound meaning. Some things are taken externally; some are received within; but the food of the body has analogies with that of the soul. So much may be said at the moment of certain aspects which encompass the literature of the Graal, as the hills stand round Jerusalem. The four Hallows are the Cup, the Lance, the Sword and the Dish, paten or patella – these four, and the greatest of these is the Cup.

As all the hallows are therefore, in a certain sense, reducible to a single hallow, so there are four epochs in the history of the Sacred

Vessel, and about these there is one question into which they are resolved. The first epoch in the history is concerned with the origin of
the Vessel; the second gives us the place and circumstances of its par-
tial manifestation; the third tells us of things within and without which
led to its removal or recession; and the fourth epoch deals ostensibly
with its departure. The texts therefore purport to provide the complete history of the Graal, including whence it came and whither it
has gone. In the present article I shall deal with these four epochs,
regarded as the institution of the Hallows, the hereditary keepers of
the Graal, the enchantments of Britain in connection with a wounded
keeper; and, lastly, the close of those times which the texts term adventurous, since when there has been silence on earth in respect of
the Holy Vessel. If there is a secret intention pervading the entire literature, it must be held to reside in these epochs; their consideration
should manifest it in part, and should enable us to deal, at the close of
the whole research, with the final problem, being that which is really
signified by the departure of the Graal.

Each of the Hallows has its implied mystery, besides that which
appears openly in its express nature, and as we know that the mysteries of God are mysteries of patience and compassion, we shall be
prepared to find in those of the Graal legend that even their offices of
judgment are formularies of concealed mercy. They are therefore both
declared and undeclared, that is to say, understood; and as there are
certain Hallows which only appear occasionally, so there are sugges-
tions and inferences concerning others which do not appear at all.
The Lance, as I have said, is that which was used the Roman soldier
Longis to pierce the side of Christ at the Crucifixion, or it is this at
least according to the general tradition. Of the Sword there are various stories: it is (a) that which was used to behead St. John the Bap-
tist, in which case we can understand its place as a sacred object; (b)
that of the King and Prophet David, committed by Solomon to a wonderful ship which went voyaging and voyaging throughout the ages,
till it should be seen by Galahad, the last scion of the Royal House of
Israel; or (c) it is simply an instrument preserved in connection with a
legend of vengeance, in which case it was brought over from folklore
and is nothing to the purpose of the Graal.

The Dish is more difficult to specify, because its almost invariable
appearance in the pageant of the high procession is accompanied by
no intelligible explanation concerning it, and although it has also its

antecedents in folklore, its mystic explanation, if any, must be sought very far away. Like the rest of the Hallows, it is described with many variations in the different books. It may be a salver of gold and precious stones, set on a silver cloth and carried by two maidens, a goodly plate of silver, or a little golden vessel, and this simply, except in the great prose Perceval which, as it multiplies the Hallows so it divides their ministry; but here, as elsewhere, the Dish does not apparently embody the feeding properties which are one aspect of the mystery. As to these, in speaking of everything shortly, which I am compelled to do, I can state only that what was filled was the heart of man and what was reflected was the entire soul. At the close of our studies we shall find a better explanation concerning it than that of antecedents in folklore, though it will acknowledge these antecedents.

II - THE HEREDITARY KEEPERS OF THE HALLOWS.

The true legitimacies are for the most part in exile, or otherwise with their rights in abeyance. The real canons of literature can be uttered only behind doors, or in the secrecy of taverns. The secrets of the great orthodoxies are very seldom communicated, even to epopts on their advancement. The highest claims of all are not so much wanting in warrant as wanting those spokesmen who are willing to utter them. We shall not be surprised therefore to find that the custodians of the Holy Graal, which was a mystery of all secrecy, "there were no sinner can be," despite the kingly titles ascribed to them, abode in the utmost seclusion.

Let us seek in the first instance to realize the nature and place of that castle or temple which, according to the legend, was for a period of centuries the sanctuary of the Sacred Vessel and of the other hallowed objects connected therewith. We have seen that the Vessel itself was brought from Salem to Britain, and it follows from the historical texts that the transit had a special purpose, one explanation of which will be found ready to our hand when the time comes for its consideration. The castle is described after several manners, the later romances being naturally the more specific, and we get in fine a geographical location. In some of the earlier legends the place is so withdrawn that it is neither named nor described. Even the late Merlin texts say merely that the Holy Vessel is in the west, that is, in the land of Vortigern, or that it abides in Northumbria. On the other hand, the temple in the German cycle is completely spiritualized; it has almost ceased to be a house made with hands, though the description on the external side is almost severe in its simplicity. In the Chretien portion of the Conte del Graal, Perceval discovers the castle in a valley, wherein it is well and beautifully situated, having a four-square tower with a principal hall in front of it, while a bridge leads up to the chief entrance. The section which is referable to Gautier de Doulens describes it as situated on a causeway tormented by the sea. The building is of vast extent and is inhabited by a great folk. In a word, we are already in the region of imaginative development and adornment. The prose Lancelot is in better correspondence with Chretien, representing the castle as situated at the far end of a great valley, with water encircling it. The most decorative account is, however, in the great prose Perceval, where the castle is reached by means of three bridges which are horrible to cross. Three great waters run below them, the first bridge being a bow-shot in length and not more than a foot in width. This is the Bridge of the Eel; but it proved wide and a fair throughway in the act of crossing. The second bridge is of ice, feeble and thin, and is arched high above the water. It is transformed on passing into the richest and strangest ever seen, and its abutments are full of images. The third and last bridge stands on columns of marble. Beyond it there is a sculptured gate, giving upon a flight of steps, which leads to a spacious hall painted with figures in gold. When Perceval visited the castle a second time he found it encompassed by a river, which came from the Earthly Paradise; it proceeded through the forest beyond as far as the hold of a hermit, where it found peace in the earth. To the castle itself there were three names attributed: The Castle of Eden, the Castle of Joy and the Castle of Souls. In conclusion as to this matter, the location, in fine, is Corbenic, which our late redaction of the Grand St. Graal mentions specifically, and which, all doubtful clouds of enchantment notwithstanding, looms almost as a landmark in the Lancelot and the Quest of Galahad. So did the place of the mysteries, from a dim and vague allusion, become

> A wilderness of building, sinking far
> And self-withdrawn into a wondrous depth
> Far sinking into splendor.

We can scarcely say whether that which had begun on earth was assumed into the spiritual place, or whether the powers and virtues from above descended to brood thereon.

I have left over from this consideration all reference to another spiritual place, in Sarras on the confines of Egypt, where the Graal, upon its outward journey, dwelt for a period and whither, after generations and centuries, it also returned for a period. As this was not the point of its origin, so it was not that of its rest; it was a stage in the passage from Salem and a stage in the transit to heaven. What was meant by this infidel city, which was yet so strangely consecrated, is hard to determine, but its consideration belongs to a later stage. It is too early again to ask what are the implicits of the great prose Perceval when it identifies the Castle of the Graal with the Earthly Paradise and the Place of Souls, but we may note it as a sign of intention, and we shall meet with it in another connection where no one has thought to look for it.

Such was the abode of the Hailows; and those who dwelt therein, the succession of Graal Keepers, belong to that order which we should expect in such precincts. Joseph of Arimathaea, the first guardian of the Vessel, passes from the scene before it has found its sanctuary. According to the Lesser Chronicles, he was succeeded by his son-in-law Brons; but according to the Greater Chronicles, as I have termed them, he was succeeded by his own son, the second Joseph, who is unknown to the other cycle. The Lesser Chronicles bridge the centuries between that generation which saw the Ascension of Christ and that which was to behold the flower of chivalry in Arthur, by means of a single keeper, who was to remain on earth till he had seen his grandson Perceval and had communicated to him the secret words pronounced at the sacrament of the Graal, which he had learned from Joseph. Perceval is the third who counts in the line of election to complete the human trinity of Graal guardians, reflecting, after their own mystic manner, those Three who bear witness in Heaven, namely, The Divine Trinity. To accomplish the hero's geniture, Alain, the son of Brons, although he had accepted celibacy, married, in some undeclared manner, and it was as his issue that Perceval was born in the fullness of the adventurous times.

From one point of view, the succession in respect of the Greater Chronicles involves fewer difficulties, because it exhibits a rudimentary sense of chronology and develops in consequence a long line of successive custodians. They are, however, quite shadowy and exist only to bridge the gulf of time. It serves no purpose to enumerate them, and I will speak therefore only of the alternative keepers who were in evidence during the days of quest. We have thus passed at one step all that period represented by the Lesser and Greater Holy Graal, by the Early History of Merlin and by the reign of Vortigern. Nor shall we be retarded by the later Merlin, according to either re-cension, after which there are only the quests, including the romance of Lancelot, but so far only as it enters into the time of the quests. On the one side, there is Brons, to whom succeeded Perceval, at the close of a life of search; on the other, there is the King Pelles, lord of the Castle Corbenic, whose daughter Helayne gave Galahad as issue to Lancelot, himself a lineal descendant of the King reigning at Sarras in the days of Joseph of Arimathaea and the first flight of the Graal. Galahad was the last keeper recognized by this cycle, and he seems to have been appointed only for the purpose of removing the Vessel. It was: *Ite, missa est,* and *est consummatum,* when he died and rose to the stars.

III - THE ENCHANTMENTS OF BRITAIN AND THE KING'S WOUNDING.

We have seen that, according to the High History of Perceval, the great and secret sanctuary gave upon the Earthly Paradise, even as the visible world gives upon the world unseen; and there will be no question for us that its external splendor signifies the soul within, even as the outward beauties of Nature are the vestures of the high graces which communicate under indefectible warrants to those in-stituted sacraments which exceed Nature. This manner of doctrine, put forward evasively in story-books, while the Orthodox Church stood aloof but vigilant and dubious, is enough in the way of won-ders; but we have now to consider how a horror fell upon the Secret House of God and a subtle work of sorcery on the world which en-compassed it. No one knew better than the old makers of romance that the places of enchantment are places of high seeming and not of realities situated in time and space; they were not therefore dealing in common legendary lore; but were plying, if I may so express it, some secret trade, which may perhaps disclose its nature in the light of events externally, or, this failing, in that more obscure light which shines about the precincts of other coincident mysteries – a possibility which bears the greater aspect of likelihood because the fact that the Graal, throughout the romances, is uniformly described as a mystery must render it a tolerable thesis that it can be explained by other mysteries, if any such were prevalent at the same time in the same countries of Europe.

The nature of the horror within, which I have termed already a certain cloud upon the sanctuary, is described after several manners. In one cycle, the flesh, which at no time profits anything, has smitten deeply into the life of the Keeper; in another, he is unable to die till he has seen the last scion of his house and has communicated to him certain secret words; in yet another, which on the surface is void of meaning, he is suffering more especially from his great age; he has alternatively received a dolorous stroke from a sword-thrust; and as a final explanation there is that of a mystic question which should have been asked and was not for a period of many years. These things are reflected upon the order without, sometimes, as it would seem, only in the immediate neighborhood of the castle; more generally on the whole of Britain; while in rare instances the world itself is involved, at least by imputation. The quality of the enchantment is sometimes a suspension of Nature in her common operations; sometimes it approaches a frenzy which leads knights to destroy each other, which rifles maids and matrons, and so forth. In the legends of Perceval and Gawain the healing depends on the asking, in fine, of the question, which restores Nature to her proper course and the sense of sanity to chivalry. In the great quest of Galahad, owing to continuous editing, there is some confusion regarding the King's wounding; the enchantment without is replaced by the notion of certain times of adventure; and there is no interrogation which can be identified with that of the other traditions. There is, however, a dual healing, that of the Keeper of the Graal in those versions of the text which show clearly that he was wounded, and that of another personage, whose sin dates back to the first times of the legend, being one of unprepared intrusion into the most secret mysteries of the Graal. We have otherwise the whole process of the Quest lifted into a high spiritual region, the implicits of which will provide us at a later stage with the master-key of the mystery.

IV - THE REMOVAL OF THE HALLOWS.

A distinction in the Graal literature between Quest versions and versions of Early History is known to scholarship in England, and though it is not quite definite in itself, it can be adapted in our interest. Speaking of the first class, the keynote of the Perceval quest is the suppression of a certain word and this, as we shall see, at first causes dire misery, postponing the advancement of the hero; but in the end it makes perhaps for his further recognition and ensures his more perfect calling, so that he is crowned in fine as he would not have been crowned at first. On the other hand, the keynote of the historical series, to make use of the expression in a sense that is not usually attached to it, is: A, the suppression or concealment of that potent sacramental formula, in the absence of which, as we have seen already, the office of the Christian ministry is not indeed abrogated but is foreshortened or substituted, so that there is something of an extra-valid character wanting to the external sanctuaries; B, the removal, cessation, or assumption of a certain school of ordination which held from heaven the highest warrants, but itself ordained no one; and the substitution thereafter of some other mode of succession, venerable enough in its way and the next surviving best after the abrogation of the old, but not the high actuality of all, not the evidence of things unseen made physically and spiritually manifest as the term of faith.

Seeing now that the great sacraments do not pass away, it must follow that in the removal of the Holy Graal, as it is narrated in the texts, we are in the presence of another mystery of intention which appears the most obscure of all. The cloud that dwelt on the sanctuary, the inhibition which was on the world without, the hurt almost past healing which overtook the hereditary keeper, are ample evidence in themselves that evil had entered into the holy place, despite all the warrants which it held and all the graces and hallows which dwelt therein. With one curious exception, the keeper was, in fine, healed; the enchantment was also removed; and the achievement of the last Warden, at least in some instances, must have been designed, after a certain manner and within a certain measure, to substitute a greater glory for the cloud on the secret sanctuary. All this notwithstanding, the end of the great quests, the term of the whole mystery, was simply the removal thereof. It occurs in each romance under different circumstances, and it was not, as we shall learn, always of an absolute kind. In the Conte del Graal it is said that it was taken away, possibly to heaven, a statement which also obtains in respect of the alternative ending supplied by Gerbert; in the Didot Perceval it was seen no more; in the great prose Perceval it was distributed, so far as we can tell, with the other Hallows, to certain hermits, and it ceased simply to manifest; in Wolfram the whole question is left open in perpetuity, for at the close of the poem the keeper remains alive; in the Titurel of Albert von Schaffenberg the Vessel was carried eastward into the dubious realm of Prester John, and there apparently it remains; in the quest of Galahad it is assumed by Heaven itself, and the last keeper followed; but, in spite of this, the lost recension, as represented, faithfully or otherwise, by the Welsh Quest, says that though it was not seen so openly, it was seen once by Sir Gawain, the least prepared and least warranted of all the Graal seekers, whose quest, moreover, was for the most part rather accidental than intended.

Speaking now from the mystic standpoint, the removal of the Holy Graal has in a certain sense the characteristics of an obscure vengeance. The destruction of the external order would appear to have been decreed. The Graal is carried away and its custodians are translated. The removal certifies the withdrawal of an object which we know, mystically speaking, is never taken away. In respect of its imputed removal, it is taken thither where it belongs; it is the same story as that of the Lost Word in Masonry. It is that which in departing hence draws after it all that belongs thereto. In other words, it goes before the cohort of election as the Pillars of Fire and Cloud before Israel in the Wilderness. The root and essence of the matter can be put shortly in these words: The Graal was not taken away, but it went to its own place, which is that of every man.

The Galahad Quest closes the canon of the literature. Other romances have said that the Sacred Vessel was not seen so openly, or that it was heard of no more, or that it had passed into concealment, and so forth; but this crowning legend carries it into complete transcendence, amidst appropriate ceremonial, though otherwise it leaves the Arthurian sacrament sufficiently unfinished. That is to say, it is still to be communicated for the last time to the whole world on the return of Arthur. The Graal is in hiding, like Arthur; but the Graal is, like Arthur, to return. Meanwhile, the chivalry of the world is broken, and the kingdom is destroyed. The master of all chivalry has received in his turn a dolorous stroke and is removed through a mist of enchantment, under dubious wardens, to the land of the setting sun, even into an exile of the ages. But he also is to be in fine healed and to return, though at what time we know not, for centuries pass as days, within the certain knowledge of Ogier the Dane. So much as this may perhaps be hazarded on the point of time, namely, that the King's rendering shall be when the King's dark barge, sailing westward, like the lighter craft of Hiawatha, shall meet with the Graal, which set forth eastward, since the Graal must heal the King, and these shall meet truly when justice and mercy kiss. The Graal is not therefore lost, but gone before.

Pillars of the Temple

LET the student recall in the first place his experience with two figurative Pillars in the Craft Grades of Masonry, how the significance of one is explained to him at the beginning of his life of brotherhood, and that of the second at the next stage of his progress. The importance attributed to both is of that kind precisely which would lead him to expect that he might hear further and more definitely concerning them in some later grade of his advancement. Such, however, is not the case : they pass out of sight completely and he is left at a loose end, wondering perhaps why they have been introduced to his notice in this very express manner, or-with a better gift of reflection-concluding tentatively that he may be said to stand between them as on the threshold of the MASTER GRADE and to issue between them into that Temple built of old, about which he hears in the central legend of the Craft. He has otherwise finished with them for ever, not only within the measures of the Craft but in the several sequences of High Grades which are in general Knowledge and activity among us. We meet with this kind of inconsequence in all the Ritual Departments. A curtain is drawn for a moment upon a prospect which looks practicable, but it falls again suddenly, and the Candidate does not enter therein. It is as if something were proposed in the mind of makers of Ritual from which they were diverted afterwards, leaving their design unfinished.

Hiram, the Widow's Son, – Now, the source of the symbolism is I KINGS vii. 13-22, the artificer concerned being Hiram, described as "a widow's son of the tribe of Naphtali," whom Solomon sent and fetched out of Tyre. "He cast two Pillars of brass, of eighteen cubits high apiece.... And he made two chapiters of molten brass, to set upon the tops of the Pillars: the height of the one chapiter was five cubits, and the height of the other chapiter was five cubits. And nets of checker work and wreaths of chain work, for the chapiters.... And two rows..... to cover the chapiters... with pomegranates.... And the chapiters... were of lily work.... And he set up the Pillars in the Porch of the Temple: and he set up the right Pillar, and called the name thereof Jachin: and he set lip the left Pillar, and called the name thereof Boaz..... . So was the work of the Pillars finished" See also 2 CHRONICLES iii. 15-17.

Jachin and Boaz. – On this text the Kabalistic treatise, entitled GATES OF LIGHT, comments as follows: "He who knows the mysteries of the two Pillars, which are Jachin and Boaz, shall understand after what manner the Neshamoth, or Minds, descend with the Ruachoth, or Spirits, and the Nephasoth, or Souls, through El-chai and Adonai by the influx of the said two Pillars." It is an allegory of the descent of spiritual man from the Supernal World into Malkuth, the kingdom of this world, which apart from human intelligence is said to be void- "even as the poor man who possesses nothing." It is said, also, that as a result of this descent there shall be built the city of Zion, which is Jerusalem- that is to say, a spiritual city, a house not made with hands, such as Masons are held to build in their hearts. In the Kabalistic Tree of Life Ckokmah and Binah are the entablatures of the two Pillars, Chesed and Geburah are the chapiters, while the bodies of the Pillars represent Netzach and Hod. "By these two Pillars and by El-chai the Minds and Spirits and Souls descend, as by their passages or channels."

Parts of the Soul.-It should be understood that Neshama = Mind is the superior grade of the soul in man; Ruach = Spirit is the rational faculty; and Nephesh = Soul is *anima vivens et vitalis*, i.e., sensitive life. The reference is not therefore to three classes of spiritual being, but to three aspects of individual human life. El-chai signifies Living God, and is that title of Divinity which is connected with Yesod. The meaning of the word Jachin is indicated in the commentary to represent that power which establishes or imprints form upon the formless, and is understood especially of the formation of man and his members, whence it is said, in DEUTERONOMY xxxii. 6: "Hath He not made thee and formed thee?" The significance of Boaz is to be sought in PSALM lxviii. 35: "He that giveth strength and power," because Boaz receives its strength from Geburah and its vigor from Binah. As regards the two Pillars taken conjointly, they are connected with the SONG OF SOLOMON v.15: "His legs are as pillars of marble, set upon sockets of fine gold." It is affirmed finally that "whosoever advances in the study of the Written and Oral Laws... . unites the Blessed Name and the mystery of Jachin and Boaz."

The Secret of Israel. – The mind of Israel has been always the mind of the Mysteries, and the secret of Israel is also a secret of initiation. It is for this reason – as I think – that Jewry produced Christianity, even as the city of this world is the material of the Mystic City. If we take in succession the symbolical stages through which a Masonic Candidate advances in the course of his progress through the authentic Rites and Grades, we shall find that farther light concerning them is derivable from Kabalistic literature, and especially from that vast work which I have named under the title of ZOHAR, together with its supplements and dependencies. The Kabalistic system of theosophy proposes Four Worlds, those of pure Deity, of Creation, Formation and of things material and inframaterial – understood as the World of Action and its recrementa. Each of these worlds is comprised in the conventional scheme which is called the Tree of Life, though it includes three Pillars, which are actually those of Wisdom, Strength and Beauty, though they are usually misplaced in Masonry. That on the right – as an observer faces the Tree – is termed the Pillar of Mercy; on the left is the Pillar of Severity, and in the middle that of Benignity. Above is the World of Deity. Through these Pillars, as by paths leading to an Eternal Sanctuary, the soul is supposed to pass till it reaches the Divine End. But that which returns to the Divine is that also which came forth therefrom- as the conception of emanation assumes – and this theosophy suggests that the divine and intellectual principles which constitute the complete man descended or were evolved through the Pillar of Mercy, to be manifested at the end of the emanation in that which is termed the Kingdom, being this present external world. Through the Pillar of Severity the written and oral law – or the Jewish Scriptures and their secret explanation – are supposed to have descended in their turn and to have been manifested ultimately on this earth. The redemption of humanity takes place through the Pilar of Benignity, signifying that the soul enters into salvation by going back on the paths which it has travelled. This scheme recalls the great parable of Pausanias concerning the Grades of Venus. The Tree of Life signifies the mystery of man's origin and his return whence he came.

A Way of Going Back. – The true method of that return is and can be the only field of research which is covered by the real Mysteries, It is the chief subject of Kabalism, and some reflections therefrom are found in Masonic Ritual. I do not suggest that Masonry is a qualified Kabalism; crudities of this kind are offences of a bygone day; but it is substantially certain that the anonymous craftsmen who elaborated the Craft Degrees had some vestiges of knowledge concerning the theosophy evolved in Jewry outside the Law and the Prophets.

Some Aspects of the Graal Legend

I.- THE INTIMATIONS AND SUGGESTIONS OF SUBSURFACE MEANING.

THE study of a great literature should begin like the preparation for a royal banquet, not without some solicitude for right conduct in the King's palace – which is the consecration of motive – and not without recollection of that source from which the most excellent gifts derive in their season to us all. Surely the things of earth are profitable only in so far as they assist us towards the things which are eternal. In this respect there are many helpers, even as the sands of the sea. The old books help us, perhaps above most things, and among them the old chronicles and the great antique legends. If the hand of God is in history it is also in folklore. We can scarcely fail of our term, since lights, both close at hand and in the unlooked-for places, kindle everywhere about us. It is difficult to say any longer that we walk in the Shadow of Death when the darkness is sown with stars.

Now, there are a few legends which may be said to stand forth among the innumerable traditions of humanity, wearing upon them the external signs and characters of some secret or mystery within them which belongs, as it would seem, rather to eternity than to time. They are in no sense connected with one another – unless indeed by certain roots which are scarcely in time and place – and yet, by a suggestion which is deeper than any suggestion of the senses, it would appear as if each were appealing to each, one bearing testimony to another, and all recalling all. They might be broken fragments of some primitive revelation which, except in these legends, has passed out of written records and far from the memory of man. The fullness of their original design may be, and sometimes is, reconstructed from age to age, but the result bears always, and that of necessity, the tincture of its particular period, reflecting the first intention sometimes in a glass darkly and sometimes in a crystal brightly, so that it is less or more, according to the mind of the age. To the class of which I am speaking belongs the Graal Legend, which in all its higher aspects may be included among the legends of the soul. Perhaps I should say rather that, when it is properly understood, the Graal is not a legend but a personal history.

It will be intelligible from this one statement that I am not putting forward a thesis for the instruction of scholarship, which is otherwise and fully equipped, and it may be desirable to make it plain from the beginning that my offering to the consideration of the literature is intended for those who have either found their place within the sanctuary of the mystic life or are at least in the outer circles. I take up the subject where it has been left by the students of folklore and by all that which might term itself authorized scholarship. *Ut adeptis appareat me illis parem et fratrem,* I have made myself acquainted with the criticism of the cycle and I am familiar with the cycle itself. It is with the texts, however, that we shall be concerned, or at least more especially, and I approach them from a new standpoint. As to thls, it win be better to specify from the outset its various particulars as follows: (I) the appropriation of certain myths and legends which are held to be pre-Christian in the root-matter, and their penetration by an advanced form of Christian Symbolism carried to a particular term; (2) the evidence of three fairly distinct sections or schools, the diversity of which is less, however, in the fundamental part of their subject than in the extent and mode of its development; (3) the connexion of this mode and of that form with other schools of symbolism, the evolution of which was going on at the same period as that of the Graal literature; (4) the close analogy in respect of the root-matter between the catholic literature of the Holy Graal and that which is connoted by the term Mysticism; (5) the traces through Graal romance and other coincident literatures of a hidden school in Christianity which, because it is an expression that has been used for over a century, I shall continue to call the Secret Church, though it predicates an instituted office that, I think, scarcely belongs to the unmanifested company with which it will be seen that I am concerned. Perhaps, within the admitted forms of expression, the idea corresponds more closely with that which is understood by the school of the prophets, though the term only describes a certain highly advanced state by one of the gifts which may be taken to belong thereto. This, I should add, is on an express assumption that the gift has little connexion with the external meaning of prophecy; it is not the power of seeing forward, but rather of sight within. In subjects of this kind, as in other subjects, the greater naturally includes the lesser, it being of minor importance to discern, for example, the coming of Christ in a glass of vision than to understand, either before or after, the vital significance of that coming. I mention this instance because it enables me to say, on the authority of my precursors, that it was out of the secret school, or company which had secured its election, that the Christ came at His season. The Graal romances are not documents of this school put forward by the external way, but are its rumors at a distance. They are not authorized; nor are they stolen; they have arisen, or the consideration of the Hidden Church follows from their consideration as something in the intellectual order connected therewith. From this point of view it is possible to collect out of the general body of the literature what I should term its intimations of subsurface meaning into a brief schedule, as follows: (a) The existence of a clouded sanctuary; (b) a great mystery; (c) a desirable communication which, except under certain circumstances, cannot take place; (d) suffering within and sorcery without; (e) supernatural grace which does not possess efficacy on the external side; (f) healing which comes from without, carrying in most cases all the signs of insufficiency and even of inhibition; (g) in fine, that which is without enters within and takes over the charge of the mystery, but it is either removed altogether or goes into deeper concealment – the outer world profits only by the removal of a vague enchantment. The unversed reader may not at the moment follow the specifics of this schedule, but if the allusions awaken his interest I can promise that they shall be made plain as we proceed.

II. - THE LITERATURE WHICH EMBODIES THE LEGEND.

The mystery of the Graal is a word which came forth out of Galilee. The literature which enshrines this mystery, setting forth the several quests which were instituted on account of it, the circumstances under which it was from time to time discovered and, in fine, its imputed removal, with all involved thereby, is one of such considerable dimensions that it may be properly described as large. This notwithstanding, there is no difficulty in presenting its broad outlines so briefly that if there be any one who is new to the subject, he can be instructed sufficiently for my purpose even from the beginning. It is to be understood, therefore, that the Holy Graal is, excepting in the German version of the legend, represented invariably as that vessel in which Christ celebrated the Last Supper and consecrated for the first time the elements of the Eucharist. According to the legend, its next use was to receive the blood from the wounds of Christ when His body was taken down from the Cross, or alternatively, from the side which was pierced by the spear of Longas. Under circumstances which are variously recounted, this vessel, its content included, was carried westward under safe guardianship, coming in fine to Britain and there remaining in the hands of successive keepers. In the days of King Arthur, the prophet and magician Merlin assumed the responsibility of carrying the legend to its term, with which object he brought about the institution of the Round Table, and the flower of Arthurian chivalry set out to find the sacred vessel. In the quests which followed, the knighthood depicted in the greater romances has become a mystery of ideality, and nothing save its feeble reflection could have been found on earth. The quests were to some extent preconceived in the mind of legend, and although a few of them were successful, that which followed was the removal of the Holy Graal. The companions of the quest asked, as one may say, for bread, and to those who were unworthy there was given the stone of their proper offence, but to others the spiritual meat which passes all understanding.

That this account instructs the uninitiated person most imperfectly will be obvious to any one who is acquainted with the great body of the literature, but, within the limits to which I have restricted it intentionally, I do not know that if it were put differently, it would be put better or more in harmony with the general sense of the romances.

The places of the legend, its reflections and its rumors, are France, England, Germany, Holland, Italy, Spain and Wales. France and England were united in respect of their literature during the Anglo-Norman period, and when this period was over England contributed nothing to the Graal cycle except renderings of French texts and one compilation therefrom. It should be further remembered that, according to the mind of scholarship, several of the Anglo-Norman texts are not extant in their original form, but have been edited and harmonized. Germany had an indigenous version of the legend, combined, by its own evidence, with a French source which is now unknown. The Dutch version is comparatively an old compilation, also from French sources; Italy is represented only by translations from the French, and these were the work of Rusticien de Pise; the inclusion of Spain is really a question of liberality, for there is no Spanish version of the Graal legend as such, or it exists only in the rare allusions of a certain romance of Merlin, which again was originally in French. As regards Wales, there is also no indigenous literature of the Graal legend, as it was understood by the French romancers, but there are certain primeval traditions and bardic remanents which are held to be the root-matter of the whole cycle, and two at least of the questing knights are found among the Mabinogion heroes. In the thirteenth century and later, the legend, as we now have it, was carried across the Marches, but it is represented by translations only. It follows that the Graal literature, as I understand the term, belongs solely to France and Germany. To these restrictions of place may be added a restriction of time, for nothing which is now extant can be dated prior to 1175, and after *circa* 1230 we have only translations and digests. The allocation of individual texts to particular dates within this period is, in certain cases, inferential and in some entirely speculative. It will be understood, therefore, that in presenting the subjoined tabulation I am not concerned with rigid priority in time but rather with affinities of intention, by which certain texts fall into defined groups. The literature may in this manner be classified into sections as follows: —

(A) The Lesser Histories or Chronicles of the Holy Graal, otherwise, the Cycle of Robert de Borron, in which is comprised: (I) The Metrical Romance of Joseph of Arimathea; (2) the Lesser Holy Graal, which is a prose version of the metrical romance as above; (3) the Early Prose Merlin, which represents a lost metrical romance, or more accurately a poem of which 500 lines alone remain extant; (4) the Didot Perceval, so called after the designation of the only manuscript by which it is known; it presents one version of the search after the Holy Graal, as distinguished from its legendary history and the connections thereof.

The characteristics in common of these four romances, by which they are grouped into a cycle, are: (I) The idea that certain secret words were transmitted from Apostolic times and were carried from East to West; (2) the succession of Brons as Keeper of the Holy Graal immediately after Joseph of Arimathea.

(B) The Greater Chronicles of the Holy Graal, comprising: (I) The Saint Graal, or Joseph of Arimathea, called also the first branch of the Romances of the Round Table and the Grand or Greater Holy Graal; (2) the later prose romances of Merlin, being that which, because it is more widely diffused, has been sometimes termed the Vulgate, and that which is known as the Huth Merlin, following the designation of the only extant manuscript; (3) the great prose Lancelot; (4) the great prose Perceval le Gallois, an alternative version of the quest, known also in English as the High History of the Holy Graal; (5) the Quest of the Holy Graal, called also the last book of the Round Table, containing the search and achievement of Galahad. From my standpoint this is the quest *par excellence*.

It should be understood that the great prose Perceval and the great quest of Galahad exclude one another, so that they stand as alternatives in the tabulation. The characteristics of this cycle are: (I) The succession of a second Joseph as Keeper of the Holy Graal immediately after his father, Joseph of Arimathea, and during the latter's lifetime, this dignity not being conferred upon Brons, either then or later; (2) the substitution of a claim in respect of apostolic succession for that of a secret verbal formula.

(C) The Conte del Graal, otherwise, the Perceval le Gallois of Chretien de Trotes, being the metrical romance which comprises the quests of Perceval and Gawain. It was successively continued by several later poets, some of whose versions are alternative and exclusive of one another. The Conte del Graal is the largest document of the Anglo-Norman cycle.

(D) The German cycle, comprising: (I) The Parsifal of Wolfram von Eschenbach; (2) the Titurel of Albrecht von Schaffenberg; (3) Diu Cronely Henrich von dem Turlin; (4) the Lancelot of Ulrich du Zazikhoven.

The dominant text of the German cycle is that of Wolfram, which is almost generically distinct from the histories and quests offered by the Anglo-Norman versions. At the moment it will be sufficient to say that it represents the Holy Graal as in the custody of a knightly company which, both expressly and by inference, recalls the order of the Knights Templar. As a final consideration in respect of all the cycles, it may be added that the romantic literature of chivalry diminishes in consequence and interest in proportion as it is removed from the Arthurian motive and period. It does not matter how remote the connection may be, there is still the particular atmosphere. The Carlovingian cycle in comparison is mere indiscrimination and violence. There are no books in the manner of chivalry to compare with *The Morte d'Athur, The High History of Perceval* and *The Quest of the Haut Prince Galahad after the Holy Graal.*

III - THE IMPLICITS OF THE MYSTERY.

There are several literatures which exhibit with various degrees of plainness the presence of that subsurface meaning to which I have referred in respect of the Graal legends; but there as here, so far as the outward text is concerned, it is suggested rather than affirmed. This additional sense may underlie the entire body of a literature, or it may be merely some concealed intention or a claim put forward evasively. The subsurface significance of the Graal legends belongs mainly to the second class. It is from this point of view that my departure is here made, and if it is a warrantable assumption, some at least of the literature will, expressly or otherwise, be found to contain these elements in no uncertain manner. As a matter of fact, we shall find them, though it is rather by the way of things which are implied, or which follow as inferences, but they are not for this reason less clear or less demonstrable. The implicits of the Graal literature are indeed more numerous than we should expect to meet with at the period in books of the western world. I believe them to exceed, for example, those which are discoverable in the alchemical writings of the late twelfth or early thirteenth century, though antecedently we might have been prepared to find them more numerous in the avowedly secret books of Hermetic adepts. In a single section of a paper which is short of necessity I can deal only with those which are most important, leaving to a later period any additional examples which may transpire as the inquiry proceeds.

The explicit in chief of that cycle which I have termed the Lesser Histories or Chronicles of the Holy Graal is that certain secret words were communicated to Joseph of Arimathea by Christ Himself, and that these must remain in reserve, being committed from Keeper to Keeper by the oral method only. On the other hand, the implicit of Robert de Borron's poem resides in the question as to what he understood by their office. In the Lesser Holy Graal the implicit of the metrical romance passes into actual expression, and it becomes more clear in this manner that the secret words were those used by the custodians of the Holy Graal in the consecration of the elements of the Eucharist.

When the Greater Holy Graal was produced as an imputed branch of Arthurian literature, there is no need to say that the Roman Pontiff was then as now, at least in respect of his claim, the first bishop of Christendom, and, by the evidence of tradition at least, he derived from St. Peter, who was *episcopus primus et pontifex primordialis*. This notwithstanding, the romance attributes the same title to a son of Joseph of Arimathea, who is called the Second Joseph, and here is the first suggestion of a concealed motive therein. The Greater Holy Graal and the metrical romance of De Borron are the texts in chief of their particular cycles, and it does not follow, or at least in all cases, that their several continuations or derivatives are extensions of the implicits which I have mentioned. In the first case, the early prose Merlin has an implied motive of its own which need not at the moment detain us, and the Didot Perceval is manifestly unauthentic as a sequel, by which I mean that it does not represent the mind of the earlier texts, though it has an importance of its own and also its own implicits. On the other hand, in what I have termed the Greater Chronicles of the Holy Graal there is, if possible, a more complete divergence in respect of the final document, and I can best explain it by saying that if we can suppose for a moment that the Grand Saint Graal was produced in the interests of a Pan-Britannic Church, or alternatively of some secret school of religion, then the Great Prose Quest, or Chronicle of Galahad, would represent an interpretation on the part of the orthodox church to take over the literature. At the same time, the several parts of each cycle under consideration belong thereto and cannot be located otherwise. The further divisions under which I have scheduled the body- general of the literature, and especially the German cycle, will be considered at some length in their proper place, when their explicit and implied motives will be specified; for the present it will be sufficient to say that they do not put forward the claims with which I am now dealing, namely, the secret formula in respect of the De Borron cycle and a super-apostolic succession in respect of the Greater Holy Graal, with that which derives therefrom. As regards both claims, we must remember that although we are dealing with a department of romantic literature, their content does not belong to romance; the faculty of invention in stories is one thing, and I think that modem criticism has made insufficient allowance for its spontaneity, yet through all the tales of chivalry it worked within certain lines. It would not devise secret Eucharistic words or put forward strange claims which almost make void the Christian apostolate in favor of some unheard of succession communicated directly from Christ after Pentecost. We know absolutely that this kind of machinery belongs to another order. If it does not, then the apocryphal gospels were imbued with the romantic spirit, and the explanation of Manichean heresy may be sought in a flight of verse.

I suppose that what follows from the claims has not entered into the consciousness of official scholarship, because it is otherwise concerned, but it may have entered already into the thought of those among my readers whose preoccupations are similar to my own, and I will now state it in a summary manner. As the secret words of consecration, the true words which have to be pronounced over the sacramental elements so that they may be converted into the true Eucharist, have, by the hypothesis, never been expressed in writing, it follows that since the Graal was withdrawn from the world, together with its custodians, the Christian Church has had to be content with what it has, namely, a substituted sacrament. And as the super- apostolic succession, also by the hypothesis, must have ceased from the world when the last Keeper of the Graal followed his vessel into heaven, the Christian Church has again been reduced to the ministration of some other and apparently lesser succession.

If I were asked to adjudicate on the value of such claims, I should say that the doctrine is the body of the Lord and its right understanding is the spirit. Whosoever therefore puts forward a claim on behalf of secret formula in connection with the Eucharistic rite has forgotten the one thing needful – that there are valid consecrations everywhere. The question of apostolic succession is in the same position, because the truly valid transmissions are those of grace itself, which communicates from the source of grace direct to the soul; and the essence of the sacerdotal office is that those who have received supernatural life should assist others so to prepare their ground that they may also in due season, but always from the same source, become spiritually alive. It remains, however, that the implicits with which I have been dealing are actually the implicits in chief of the Graal books, and that they do not make for harmony with the teaching of the orthodox churches does not need stating. From whence therefore and with what intention were they imported into the body of romance? Before this question can be answered we shall have to proceed much further in the consideration of the literature, but my next section can deal only with a preliminary clearance of the ground. As a conclusion to the present part, let me add that any scheme of interpretation which fails to account for the claim to a super-efficacious Eucharistic consecration and a super-apostolic succession accounts for very little that is important in the last resource. It is in this sense that I take up the subject at the point where it has been left by scholarship, considering these problems in the light of all that can be gathered from the texts themselves, from certain coincident literatures, and from the theological and historical position of the Celtic Church, as a preliminary to the consideration in fine which I have already indicated by my reference to a secret school existing within the Church, or at least to be approached intellectually more readily from this direction.

IV. - SOME ANTECEDENTS IN FOLKLORE.

The beginnings of literature are like the beginnings of life – questions of antecedents which are past finding out, and perhaps they do not signify vitally on either side, because the keys of all mysteries are to be sought in the comprehension of their term, rather than in their initial stages. Modem scholarship lays great and indeed exclusive stress on the old Celtic antecedents of the Graal literature, and on certain Welsh and other prototypes of the Perseval Quest in which the sacred vessel does not appear at all. As regards these affiliations, whether Welsh, English, or Irish, I do not think that sufficient allowance has been made for the following facts: (a) That every fiction and legend depends, as already suggested, from prior legend and fiction; (b) that the antecedents are both explicit and implicit, intentional or unconscious, just as in these days we have wilful and undesigned imitation; (c) that the persistence of legends is by the way of their transfiguration. We have done nothing to explain the ascension of the Graal to heaven and the assumption of Galahad when we have ascertained that some centuries before there were myths about the Cauldron of Ceridwen or that of the Dagda, any more than we have accounted for Christianity if we have ascertained, and this even indubitably, that some ecclesiastical ceremonial is an adaptation of pre-Christian rites. Here, as in so many other instances, the essence of everything resides in the intention. If I possess the true apostolic succession, then, *ex hypothesi* at least, I do not the less consecrate the Eucharist if I use the Latin rite, which expresses the act of Christ in the past tense, or some archaic oriental rite, which expressed it in the present.

There is in any case no question as to the Graal antecedents in folklore; and I should be the last to minimize their importance after their own kind, just as I should not abandon the official Church because I had been received into the greater Church which is within. I believe personally that the importance has been unduly magnified because it has been taken by scholarship for the all in all of its research. But there is plenty of room for every one of the interests, and as that which I represent does not interfere with anything, which has become so far vested, I ask for tolerance regarding it. My position is that the old myths were taken over for the purposes of Christian symbolism, under the influence of a particular but not an expressed motive, and it was subsequently to this appropriation that they assumed importance. It is, therefore, as I may say, simply to clear the issues that I place those of my readers who may feel concerned with the subject in possession of the bare elements which were carried from pre-Christian time into the Graal mythos, as follows: —

I. We hear of an Irish legend concerning the Cauldron of the Dagda, from which no company ever went away unsatisfied. It was one of the four talismans which a certain godlike race brought with them when they first came into Ireland. As the particular talisman in question, though magical, was not spiritual, it is useless to our purpose; but it connects with the palmary hallow of the Graal mystery, because that also was food-giving, though this property was the least of its great virtues, just as the stone of transmutation by alchemy was classed among the least possessions of the Rosicrucian Fraternity.

2. There is the Cauldron of Bendigeid Vran, the son of Llyr, in one of the old Welsh Mabinogion, the property of which, says one story, is that if a man be slain today and cast therein, tomorrow he will be as well as he ever was at the best, except that he will not regain his speech. He remains, therefore, in the condition of Perceval when that hero of the Graal stood in the presence of the mystery with a spell of silence upon him. Except in so far as the Cup of the Graal legend concerns a mystery of speech and its suppression, it is difficult to trace its correspondence with this cauldron, which I should mention, however, came into Wales from Ireland. It so happens that institutions of analogy are made sometimes by scholarship on warrants which they would be the first to repudiate if the object, let us say, were to establish some point advanced by a mystic. I do not reject them, and I do not intend to use similar comparisons on evidence which appears so slight; but I must place on record that the derivation, if true, is unimportant, even as it is also unimportant that Adam, who received the breath of life from the Divine Spirit, had elements of red earth which entered into his material composition. The lights which shine upon the altar are not less sacramental lights because they are also earthly wax; and though the externals are bread and wine, the Eucharist is still the Eucharist.

In addition to analogies like those which I have just cited, there are two versions of the quest or mission of Perceval into which the mystery of the Graal does not enter as a part. In their extant forms they are much later than any of the Graal literature. One is the story of Peredur the son of Evrawc in the Welsh Mabinogion, and the other is the English metrical romance of Syr Percyvelle. The Welsh Mabinogi is like the wild world before the institution of the sacraments, and from any literary standpoint it is confused and disconcerting. Scholars have compared it to the Lay of the Great Fool, and I think that the analogy obtains, not only in the Welsh fable, but also in such masterpieces of nature-born poetry as that of Chretien de Troyes. On the other hand, the English poem is a thing of no importance except in respect of its connections, and as to these it will be sufficient to say that even scholarship values it only for its doubtful traces of some early prototype which is lost.   The anticedents of the Graal legend in folklore have been a wide field for patient research, nor is that field exhausted; it has also offered an opportunity for great speculations which go to show that the worlds of enchantment are not worlds which have past like the Edomite kings; but as I know that there was a king afterwards in Israel, I have concluded at this point to abandon those quests, which for myself and those whom I represent are without term or effect, and to hold only to the matter in hand, which is the development of a sacramental and mystical cosmos in literature out of the wild elements which strove one with another, as in the time of chaos so also in pre-Christian Celtic folklore.

The Tarot:
A Wheel of Fortune

THIS is not, for once in a way – though it may seem certainly for once only – a study in withdrawn areas of mystical philosophy, nor precisely an investigation of root-matters of symbolism, nor is it even exclusively an account of divination, which in itself would suggest a sufficiently wide departure from my known and admitted concerns. Having thus stated a fact rather than opened out an apologia, I will take up the matter in hand and complete the circle, if necessary, by reverting at the end to the point at which I begin.

To the great majority of my readers, I suppose that it will be scarcely necessary to answer, by way of precaution, the hypothetical question: What then is the Tarot? Every one knows that it is a method of divination by cards, but that the cards which are used for the purpose differ in some important respects from those ordinary playing kinds which are perhaps a good deal more familiar in most homes than the things which used to be called household words. These cards are also used for fortune-telling, and the publishers of The Occult

Review have recently issued a certain Manual of Cartomancy which gives one of the modes of operation among a hundred and one curiosities for the delectation of people with occult predispositions and perhaps some intuitive faculties. The writer of the Manual, who has sufficient grace in his heart to speak of trifles only with becoming seriousness and of grave things as if he knew that strange worlds lie occasionally behind them, has included in his budget of paradoxes a long and recollected section on this very subject of the Tarot. I have myself still more recently prefaced and revised a new edition of The Tarot of the Bohemians, translated into English from the French of Dr. Papus, the head of the school of Martinism at Paris. There is once more available a work which had become scarce, and for which many have been looking there and here in the catalogues.

It follows that the Tarot is, as people say, in the air; but there is one difficulty with which we had all to contend in England. It is easy to read about the subject, and if people have the mind they may become quite learned respecting it, more especially if they are familiar with French; but the cards themselves are not too easily obtainable. They are imported from the continent, which usually produces very indifferent versions in these our modern days, and has just now nothing to offer us but a very inferior Italian pack, which any one who can be called a student would do well to avoid. A little further afield some pains may secure one of the Etteilla sets, in which, however, the symbolism has been confused by the reveries of the editor, who was firstly a professional cartomancist of his period – being the end of the eighteenth century – but secondly a virtuoso in general occult arts whose zeal was in advance of his discretion and out of all measure in respect of his learning. The Marseilles pack is very much better, but this is also not at the corner of the streets, either in the city which has given it an imprint or in the great center of Paris. Bolognese and Venetian Tarots are mentioned rather than seen.

This being the case, and recurring for a moment to the fact that the Tarot, as I have said, is in the air, while many people who divine – and a substantial minority who are students rather than dippers at random into the chances of fortune – are all in want of the cards, I have embraced an opportunity which has been somewhat of the unexpected kind and have interested a very skilful and original artist in the proposal to design a set. Miss Pamela Coleman Smith, in addition to her obvious gifts, has some knowledge of Tarot values; she has lent a sympathetic ear to my proposal to rectify the symbolism by reference to channels of knowledge which are not in the open day; and we have had other help from one who is deeply versed in the subject. The result, and for the first time on record, is a marriage of art and symbolism for the production of a true Tarot under one of its aspects; it should be understood that there are others, but whatever has transpired about them or is likely to be related hereafter is and can only be concerned with a part of hidden system and will mislead rather than direct.

The version with which I am concerned is on the eve of publication; this is therefore an advertisement concerning it, and that it may not want for boldness I produce here in their order certain specimen cards, which, on the artistic side, will – I think – speak for themselves. About their meanings a word must be said presently, and to this I will lead up by a few preliminary remarks on the debated origin of Tarot. It has been referred to India, China, Egypt, which allocations are speculative, and though presented in the terminology of certitude, they are so much fantasia. No one knows whence it came, unless, by a great dispensation, he happens to have been born in France, where there are high grades of conviction in all that belongs to the province of occultism and its history. It is in this way that the Tarot is called The Book of Thoth, the Book of Thrice Great Hermes, and because the cards themselves did not support the attribution, they have been perfected by the late editors and adorned with Egyptian characteristics. The truth is that the intimations of mystery abiding behind the Tarot have suggested too readily the conventional places of mystery; but seeing that secret doctrine – admittedly concerned therein – is of all ages and peoples and climes, remoteness of origin in time and the farthest Orient in place are not indispensable assumptions.

Now, the Tarot has twenty-two Trump-Major cards, which have no analogy with playing cards, and from these I have selected four specimens taken direct from the drawings and naturally much larger than they will appear in the color-printed set. I will speak of these in respect of their higher symbolism. Last or first, as you please, in its own series, is the card which represents Zero and is entitled The Fool. It is in no sense, though it has been called, a type of humanity as the blind slave of matter, though in the common traffic of fortune-telling it may, and does, stand for extravagance or even for enthusiasm and the folly which its name implies. It is said by Eliphas Levi to signify eternal life; it is a card of the joy of life before it has been embittered by experience on the material plane. On the spiritual plane it is the soul, also at the beginning of its experience, aspiring towards the higher things before it has attained thereto.

The first numbered Trump Major, called the Magician, is he on whom "the spark from heaven" has fallen, who draws from above and derives thence to below. Levi says that it is god in His unity and man as a reflection of God; others describe it as the Divine World and the Absolute. It is the card of illumination, and so looks the Fool when he has seen God. The second numbered Trump is the High Priestess, here beautifully depicted, with all her symbolical attributes. She has the solar cross on her breast and the lunar crescent on her head. She is called the house of God, the Sanctuary and even the Kabalah, or se- cret tradition. She is really the Great Mother and the Secret Church. The last of the Trumps Major which I present here is the nineteenth in the series, and is called the Sun as the symbol of light and revelation. It is the glory of all the worlds. The naked child mounted on the great horse is the complement by antithesis of the thirteenth card – which is Death, also mounted.

My smaller cards are designed to illustrate the Minor Arcana, and I will refer to their divinatory meanings. The King of Wands – ardent, equitable, noble – represents goodness blended with severity. The Queen of Cups signifies love and devotion, the images of which she sees like visions in her vessel. The Knight of Swords is even as Galahad on the Quest, dispersing the enemies thereof. The Page of Pentacles – a youthful figure looking at a talisman, which hovers over his raised hands – really typifies the scholar, but he is also the one who bears news. I can hardly mention the remaining numbered cards – The Six of Wands, crowned with hope and confidence; the Five of Cups, which is the card of heritage diverted and life emptied of joy; the Eight of Swords, which means disquietude, conflict, crisis, some- time fatality; the Nine of Swords, which should be compared with the former; it is the card of disappointment, well illustrated by the picture.

The meanings attributed to the Trumps Major, or Greater Arcana, when taken, as they usually are, apart from the ordinary numbered and court cards, depend upon the worlds or spheres of conscious- ness to which particular interpretations have referred them. When they are combined with the Lesser Arcana for purposes of divination, and when thus the pack forms one sequence of seventy-eight cards, each cartomancist has followed his own intuition and observation of results. The gift of second sight overrides conventions and precedents, but for those who do not possess it, or in whom it has not been developed, a summary of accepted meanings is desirable, and this I have sought to supply in the little interpretative work which accompanies the set of cards. The question remains whether there is an integral connection between the Greater and Lesser Arcana, and if this is the case how to establish their respective offices in higher Tarot symbolism. If, however, their connection is arbitrary, a separation should be effected, the Lesser Arcana being allocated to their proper place in cartomancy and the Trumps Major to their own, which is to seership of another order.

The compiler of the Manual of Cartomancy calls the Tarot the higher way to fortune, and – between the Major and Minor Arcana – if any one can so interpret it – as he and I do – let me say unto him with the Psalmist: Intende, *prospere procede et regna* [Spread out, favorably make progress and reign.] And so I return to the question of an apologia, but only to conclude that after all the Tarot is a research in symbolism; its study is a mystic experiment; and though it has been, is, and will be used for divination, it belongs to another realm and began therein. Those who desire to go further will learn how and why in my short Key to the Tarot, which accompanies the set of cards.

What is Alchemy?

PART ONE

THERE are certain writers at the present day, and there are certain students of the subject, perhaps too wise to write, who would readily, and do, affirm that any answer to the question which heads this paper will involve, if adequate, an answer to those other and seemingly harder problems – What is Mysticism ? What is the Transcendental Philosophy? What is Magic? What Occult Science? What the Hermetic Wisdom? For they would affirm that Alchemy includes all these, and so far at least as the world which lies west of Alexandria is concerned, it is the head and crown of all. Now in this statement the central canon of a whole body of esoteric criticism is contained in the proverbial nutshell, and this criticism is in itself so important, and embodies so astounding an interpretation of a literature which is so mysterious, that in any consideration of Hermetic literature it must be reckoned with from the beginning; otherwise the mystic student will at a later period be forced to go over his ground step by step for a second time, and that even from the starting point. It is proposed in the following papers to answer definitely by the help of the evidence which is to be found in the writings of the Alchemists the question as to what Alchemy actually was and is. As in other subjects, so also in this, THE UNKNOWN WORLD proposes to itself an investigation which has not been attempted hitherto along similar lines, since at the present day, even among the students of the occult, there are few persons sufficiently instructed for an inquiry which is not only most laborious in itself but is rendered additionally difficult from the necessity of expressing its result in a manner at once readable and intelligible to the reader who is not a specialist. In a word, it is required to popularize the conclusions arrived at by a singularly abstruse erudition. This is difficult – as will be admitted – but it can be done, and it is guaranteed to the readers of these papers that they need know nothing of the matter beforehand. After the little course has been completed it is believed that they will have acquired much, in fact, nothing short of a solution of the whole problem.

In the first place, let any unversed person cast about within himself, or within the miscellaneous circle of his non-mystical acquaintance, and decide what he and they do actually at the present moment understand by Alchemy. It is quite certain that the answer will be fairly representative of all general opinion, and in effect it will be somewhat as follows: "Alchemy is a pretended science or art by which the metals ignorantly called base, such as lead and iron were supposed to be, but were never really, transmuted into the other metals as ignorantly called perfect, namely, gold and silver. The *ignis fatuus* of Alchemy was pursued by many persons – indeed, by thousands – in the past, and though they did not succeed in making gold or silver, they yet chanced in their investigations upon so many useful facts that they actually laid the foundations of chemistry as it is. For this reason it would perhaps be unjust to dishonor them; no doubt many of them were rank imposters, but not all; some were the chemists of their period." It follows from this answer that this guesswork and these groupings of the past can have nothing but a historical interest in the present advanced state of chemical knowledge. It is, of course, absurd to have recourse to an exploded scientific literature for reliable information of any kind. Goldsmith and Pinnock in history, Joyce and Mangnall in general elementary science, would be preferable to the Alchemists in chemistry. If Alchemy be really included as a branch of occult wisdom, then so much the worse for the wisdom – *ex uno disce omnia*. The question what is Alchemy is then easily answered from this standpoint – it is the dry bones of chemistry, as the Occult Sciences in general are the debris of ancient knowledge, and the dust from the ancient sanctuaries of long vanished religions – at which point these papers and THE UNKNOWN WORLD itself; would perforce come to a conclusion.

There is, however, another point of view, and that is the standpoint of the occultist. It will be pardonable perhaps to state it in an occult magazine. Now, what does the student of the Occult Sciences understand by Alchemy? Of two things, one, and let the second be reserved for the moment in the interests of that simplicity which the Alchemists themselves say is the seal of Nature and art – *sigillum Natura et artis simplicitas*. He understands the law of evolution applied by science to the development from a latent into an active condition of the essential properties of metallic and other substances. He does not understand that lead as lead or that iron as iron can be transmuted into gold or silver. He affirms that there is a common basis of all the metals, that they are not really elements, and that they are resolvable. In this case, once their component parts are known the metals will be capable of manufacture, though whether by a prohibitively expensive process is another issue. Now, beyond contradiction this is a tolerable standpoint from the standpoint of modern science itself. Chemistry is still occasionally discovering new elements, and it is occasionally resolving old and so-called elements, and indeed, a common basis of all the elements is a thing that has been talked of by men whom no one would suspect of being Mystics, either in matters of physics or philosophy.

There is, however, one obviously vulnerable point about this defensive explanation of Alchemy. It is open to the test question: Can the occultist who propounds it resolve the metallic elements, and can he make gold? If not, he is talking hypothesis alone, tolerable perhaps in the bare field of speculation, but to little real purpose until it can be proved by the event. Now, THE UNKNOWN WORLD has not been established to descant upon mere speculations or to expound dreams to its readers. It will not ignore speculation, but its chief object is to impart solid knowledge. Above all it desires to deal candidly on every subject. There are occultists at the present day who claim to have made gold. There are other occultists who claim to be in communication with those who possess the secret. About neither class is it necessary to say anything at present; claims which it is impossible to verify may be none the less good claims, but they are necessarily outside evidence. So far as can be known the occultist does not manufacture gold. At the same time his defence of Alchemy is not founded on merely hypothetical considerations. It rests on a solid basis, and that is alchemical literature and history. Here his position, whether unassailable or not, cannot be impugned by his opponents, and this for the plain reason that, so far as it is possible to gather, few of them know anything of the history and all are ignorant of the literature. He has therefore that right to speak which is given only by knowledge, and he has the further presumption in his favor that as regards archaic documents those who can give the sense can most likely explain the meaning. To put the matter as briefly as possible, the occultist finds in the great text-books of Alchemy an instruction which is virtually as old as Alchemy, namely, that the metals are composite substances. This instruction is accompanied by a claim which is, in effect, that the Alchemists had through their investigations become acquainted with a process which demonstrated by their resolution the alleged fact that metals are not of a simple nature. Furthermore, the claim itself is found side by side with a process which pretends to be practical, which is given furthermore in a detailed manner, for accomplishing the disintegration in question. Thus it would seem that in a supposed twilight of chemical science, in an apparently inchoate condition of physics, there were men in possession of a power with which the most advanced applied knowledge of this nineteenth century is not as yet equipped. This is the first point in the defence of Alchemy which will be raised by the informed occultist. But, in the second place, there is another instruction to be found in these old textbooks, and that is the instruction of development- the absolute recognition that in all natural substances there exist potentialities which can be developed by the art of a skilled physicist, and the method of this eduction is pretended to be imparted by the textbooks, so that here again we find a doctrine, and connected with that doctrine a formal practice, which is not only in advance of the supposed science of the period but is actually a governing doctrine and a palmary source of illumination at the present day. Thirdly, the testimony of Alchemical literature to these two instructions, and to the processes which applied them, is not a casual, isolated, or conflicting testimony, nor again is it read into the literature by a specious method of inter-pretation; it is upon the face of the whole literature; amidst an ex-traordinary variety of formal difference, and amidst protean disguises of terminology, there is found the same radical teaching everywhere. In whatsoever age or country, the adepts on all ultimate matters never disagree- a point upon which they themselves frequently insist, re-garding their singular unanimity as a proof of the truth of their art. So much as regards the literature of Alchemy, and from this the occultist would appeal to the history of the secret sciences for convincing evi-dence that, if evidence be anything, trausmutations have taken place. He would appeal to the case of Glauber, to the case of Van Helmont, to the case of Lascaris and his disciples, to that also of Michael Sendivogius, and if his instances were limited to these it is not from a paucity of further testimony, but because the earlier examples, such as Raymond Lully, Nicholas Flamel, Bernard Trevisan, and Denis Zachaire, will be regarded as of less force and value in view of their more remote epoch. Having established these points, the occultist will proceed to affirm that they afford a sufficient warrant for the serious investigation of Alchemical literature with the object of discovering the actual process followed by the old adepts for the attainment of their singular purpose. He will frankly confess that this process still remains to be understood, because it has been veiled by its profes-sors, wrapped up in strange symbols, and disguised by a terminol-ogy which offers peculiar difficulties. Why it has been thus wilfully entangled, why it was considered advisable to make it *caviare* to the multitude, and what purpose was served by the writing of an inter-minable series of books seemingly beyond comprehension, are points which must be held over for consideration in their proper place later on. Those who, for what reason soever, have determined to study occultism, must be content to take its branches as they are, namely, as sciences that have always been kept secret. It follows from what has been advanced that the occultist should not be asked, as a test ques-tion, whether he can make gold, but whether he is warranted in tak-ing the Alchemical claim seriously, in other words, whether the lit-erature of Alchemy, amidst all its mystery, does offer some hope for its unravelment, and if on the authority of his acquaintance there-with he can, as he does, assuredly answer yes, then he is entitled to a hearing.

Now, the issue which has been dealt with hitherto in respect of Alchemy is one that is exceedingly simple. Assuming there is strong presumptive evidence that the adepts could and did manufacture the precious metals, and that they enclosed the secret of their method in a symbolic literature, it is a mere question of getting to understand the symbolism, about which it will be well to remember the axiom of Edgar Allan Poe, himself a literary Mystic, that no cryptogram invented by human ingenuity is incapable of solution by the application of human ingenuity. But there is another issue which is not by any means so simple, the existence of which was hinted at in the beginning of the present paper, and this is indeed the subject of the present inquiry. To put it in a manner so elementary as to be almost crude in presentation, there is another school of occult students who believe themselves to have discovered in Alchemy a philosophical experiment which far transcends any physical achievement. At least in its later stages and developments this school by no means denies the fact that the manufacture of material gold and silver was an object with many Alchemists, or that such a work is possible and has taken place. But they affirm that the process in metals is subordinate, and, in a sense, almost accidental, that essentially the Hermetic experiment was a spiritual experiment, and the achievement a spiritual achievement. For the evidence of this interpretation they tax the entire literature, and their citations carry with them not infrequently an extraordinary, and sometimes an irresistible, force. The exaltation of the base nature in man, by the development of his latent powers; the purification, conversion, and transmutation of man; the achievement of a hypostatic union of man with God; in a word, the accomplishment of what has been elsewhere in this magazine explained to be the true end of universal Mysticism; not only was all this the concealed aim of Alchemy, but the process by which this union was effected, veiled under the symbolism of chemistry, is the process with which the literature is concerned, which process also is alone described by all veritable adepts. The man who by proper study and contemplation, united to an appropriate interior attitude, with a corresponding conduct on the part of the exterior personality, attains a correct interpretation of Hermetic symbolism, will, in doing so, be put in possession of the secret of divine reunion, and will, so far as the requisite knowledge is concerned, be in a position to encompass the great work of the Mystics. From the standpoint of this criticism the power which operates in the transmutation of metals alchemically is, in the main, a psychic power. That is to say, a man who has passed a certain point in his spiritual development, after the mode of the Mystics, has a knowledge and control of physical forces which are not in the possession of ordinary humanity. As to this last point there is nothing inherently unreasonable in the conception that an advancing evolution, whether in the individual or the race, will give a far larger familiarity with the mysteries and the laws of the universe. On the other hand, the grand central doctrine and the supreme hope of Mysticism, that it is possible for "the divine in man" to be borne back consciously to "the divine in the universe," which was the last aspiration of Plotinus, does not need insistence in this place. There is no other object, as there is no other hope, in the whole of Transcendental Philosophy, while the development of this principle and the ministration to this desire are the chief purpose of THE UNKNOWN WORLD.

It is obvious that Alchemy, understood in this larger sense, is mystically of far higher import than a mere secret science of the manufacture of precious metals. And this being incontestable, it becomes a matter for serious inquiry which of these occult methods of interpretation is to be regarded as true. A first step towards the settlement of this problem will be a concise history of the spiritual theory. Despite his colossal doctrine of Hermetic development, nothing to the present purpose, or nothing that is sufficiently demonstrable to be of real moment, is found in the works of Paracelsus. The first traces are supposed to be imbedded in the writings of Jacob Bohme and about the same time Louis Claude de Saint Martin, the French illumine, is discovered occasionally describing spiritual truths in the language of physical chemistry. These, however, are at best but traces, very meagre and very indefinite. It was not till the year 1850, and in England, that the interpretation was definitely promulgated. In that year there appeared a work entitled A SUGGESTIVE INQUIRY INTO THE HERMETIC MYSTERY AND ALCHEMY, BEING AN ATTEMPT TO DISCOVER THE ANCIENT EXPERIMENT OF NATURE. This was a large octavo of considerable bulk; it was the production of an anonymous writer, who is now known to be a woman, whose name also is now well known, at least in certain circles, though it would be bad taste to mention it. For the peculiar character of its research, for the quaint individuality of its style, for the extraordinary wealth of suggestion which more than justifies its title, independently of the new departure which it makes in the interpretation of Hermetic symbolism, truly, this book was remarkable.

PART TWO

ELIPHAS LEVI affirms that all religions have issued from the Kabbalah and return into it; and if the term be intended to include the whole body of esoteric knowledge, no advanced occultist will be likely to dispute the statement. So far as books are concerned, it may, in like manner, be affirmed that all modern mystical literature is referable ultimately to two chief sources: on the one hand, to the wonderful books on Magic which were written by Eliphas Levi himself, and of which but a faint conception is given in the sole existing translation; and, on the other, to the "Suggestive Inquiry Concerning the Hermetic Mystery," that singular work to which reference was made last month as containing the first promulgation of the spiritual theory of Alchemy. This seems at first sight an extreme statement, and it is scarcely designed to maintain, that, for example, the Oriental doctrine of Karma is traceable in the writings of the French initiate who adopted the Jewish pseudonym of Eliphas Levi Zahed, nor that the "recovered Gnosis" of the "New Gospel of Interpretation" is borrowed from the *Suggestive Inquiry*. But these are the two chief sources of inspiration, in the sense that they have prompted research, and that it is not necessary to go outside them to understand how it is that we have come later on to have Theosophy, Christo-Theosophy, the New Kabbalism of Dr. Wynn Westcott, and the illuminations of Mrs. Kingsford. Everywhere in *Isis Unveiled* the influence of Eliphas Levi is distinctly traceable; everywhere in the Recovered Gnosis there is the suggestion of the *Inquiry*. Even the Rosicrucianism of the late Mr. Hargrave Jennings, so far as it is anything but confusion, is referable to the last mentioned work. It is doubtful if Eliphas Levi did not himself owe something to its potent influence, for his course of transcendental philosophy post dates the treatise on the Hermetic Mystery by something like ten years, and he is supposed to have accomplished wide reading in occult literature, and would seem to have known English. As it is to the magical hypotheses of the Frenchman that we are indebted for the doctrines of the astral light and for the explanations of spiritualistic phenomena which are current in theosophical circles, to name only two typical instances, so it is of the English lady that we have derived the transcendental views of alchemy, also every where now current, and not among Theosophists only. At the same time, it is theosophical literature chiefly which has multiplied the knowledge concerning it, though it does not always indicate familiarity with the source of the views. It is also to Theosophy that we owe the attempt to effect a compromise between the two schools of alchemical criticism mentioned last month, by the supposition that there were several planes of operation in alchemy, of which the metallic region was one.

Later speculations have, however, for the most part, added little to the theory as it originally stood, and the *Suggestive Inquiry* is in this respect still thoroughly representative.

To understand what is advanced in this work is to understand the whole theory, but to an unprepared student its terminology would perhaps offer certain difficulties, and therefore in attempting a brief synopsis, it will be well to present it in the simplest possible manner.

The sole connection, according to the *Suggestive Inquiry*, which subsists between Alchemy and the modern art of Chemistry is one of terms only. Alchemy is not an art of metals, but it is the Art of Life; the chemical phraseology is a veil only, and a veil which was made use of not with any arbitrary and insufficient desire to conceal for the sake of concealment, or even to ensure safety during ages of intolerance, but because the alchemical experiment is attended with great danger to man in his normal state. What, however the adepts in their writings have most strenuously sought to conceal is the nature of the Hermetic Vessel, which they admit to be a divine secret, and yet no one can intelligently study these writings without being convinced that the vessel is Man himself. Geber, for example, to quote only one among many, declares that the universal orb of the earth contains not so great mysteries and excellencies as Man reformed by God into His image, and he that desires the primacy amongst the students of Nature will no where find a greater or better subject wherein to obtain his desire than in himself, who is able to draw to himself what the alchemists call the Central Salt of Nature, who also in his regenerated wisdom possesses all things, and can unlock the most hidden mysteries. Man is, in fact, with all adepts, the one subject that contains all, and he only need be investigated for the discovery of all. Man is the true laboratory of the Hermetic Art, his life is the subject, the grand distillery, the thing distilling and the thing distilled, and self-knowledge is at the root of all alchemical tradition. To discover then the secret of Alchemy the student must look within and scrutinize true psychical experience, having regard especially to the germ of a higher faculty not commonly exercised but of which he is still in possession, and by which all the forms of things, and all the hidden springs of Nature, become intuitively known. Concerning this faculty the alchemists speak magisterially, as if it had illuminated their understanding so that they had entered into an alliance with the Omniscient Nature, and as if their individual consciousness had become one with Universal Consciousness. The first key of the Hermetic Mystery is in Mesmerism, but it is not Mesmerism working in the therapeutic sphere, but rather with a theurgic object, such as that after which the ancients aspired, and the attainment of which is believed to have been the result of initiation into the Greater Mysteries of old Greece. Between the process of these Mysteries and the process of Alchemy there is a distinctly traceable correspondence, and it is submitted that the end was identical in both cases. The danger which was the cause of the secrecy was the same also; it is that which is now connected with the Dwellers on the Threshold, the distortions and deceptions of the astral world, which lead into irrational confusion. Into this world the mesmeric trance commonly transfers its subjects, but the endeavour of Hermetic Art was a right disposition of the subject, not only liberating the spirit from its normal material bonds, but guaranteeing the truth of its experiences in a higher order of subsistence. It sought to supply a purely rational motive which enabled the subject to withstand the temptation of the astral sphere, and to follow the path upwards to the discovery of wisdom and the highest consciousness. There the soul knows herself as a whole, whereas now she is acquainted only with a part of her humanity; there also, proceeding by theurgic assistance, she attains her desired end and participates in Deity. The method of Alchemy is thus an arcane principle of self-knowledge and the narrow way of regeneration into life. Contemplation of the Highest Unity and Conjunction with the Divine Nature, the soul's consummation in the Absolute, lead up to the final stage, when the soul attains "divine intuition of that high exemplar which is before all things, and the final cause of all, which seeing only is seen, and understanding is understood, by him who penetrating all centres, discovers himself in that finally which is the source of all; and passing from himself to that, transcending, attains the end of his profession. This was the consummation of the mysteries, the ground of the Hermetic philosophy, prolific in super-material increase, transmutations, and magical effects."

It was impossible in the above synopsis, and is indeed immaterial at the moment, to exhibit after what manner the gifted authoress substantiates her theory by the evidences of alchemical literature. It is sufficient for the present purpose to summarize the interpretation of Alchemy which is offered by the *Suggestive Inquiry*.

The work, as many are aware, was immediately withdrawn from circulation; it is supposed that there are now only about twelve copies in existence, but as it is still occasionally met with, though at a very high price, in the book-market, this may be an understatement. Some ten years later, Eliphas Levi began to issue his course of initiation into "absolute knowledge," and in the year 1865 an obscure writer in America, working, so far as can be seen, quite independently of both, published anonymously a small volume of "Remarks on Alchemy and the Alchemists," in which it was attempted to show that the Hermetic adepts were not chemists, but were great masters in the conduct of life. Mr. Hitchcock, the reputed author, was not an occultist, though he had previously written on Swedenborg as a Hermetic Philosopher, and no attention seems to have been attracted by his work.

The interpretation of the *Suggestive Inquiry* was spiritual and "theurgic" in a very highly advanced degree: it was indeed essentially mystical, and proposed the end of Mysticism as that also of the Alchemical adepts. The interpretation of Eliphas Levi, who was an occultist rather than a Mystic, and does not seem to have ever really understood Mysticism, may be called intellectual, as a single citation will suffice to show.

"Like all magical mysteries, the secrets of the Great Work possess a threefold significance: they are religious, philosophical, and natural. Philosophical gold is, in religion, the Absolute and Supreme Reason; in philosophy, it is truth; in visible nature, it is the Sun; in the subterranean and mineral world, it is most pure and perfect gold. It is for this cause that the search for the Great Work is called the search after the Absolute, and that the work itself passes as the operation of the Sun. All masters of the science have recognized that material results are impossible till all the analogies of the Universal Medicine and the Philosophical Stone have been found in the two superior degrees. Then is the labor simple, expeditious, and inexpensive; otherwise, it wastes to no purpose the life and fortune of the operator. For the soul, the Universal Medicine is supreme reason and absolute justice; for the mind, it is mathematical and practical truth; for the body, it is the quintessence, which is a combination of gold and light."

The interpretation of Hitchcock was, on the other hand, purely ethical. Now, as professedly an expositor of Mysticism, THE UNKNOWN WORLD is concerned here only with the first interpretation, and with the clear issue which is included in the following question:- Does the literature of Alchemy belong to Chemistry in the sense that it is concerned with the disintegration of physical elements in the metallic order, with a view to the making of gold and silver, or is it concerned with man and the exaltation of his interior nature from the lowest to the highest condition?

In dealing with this question there is only one way possible to an exoteric inquiry like the present, and that is by a consideration of the literature and history of Alchemy. For this purpose it is necessary to begin, not precisely at the cradle of the science, because, although this was probably China, as will be discussed later on, it is a vexatious and difficult matter to settle on an actual place of origin; but for the subject in hand recourse may be had to the first appearance of Alchemy in the West, as to what is practically a starting-point.

It is much to be deplored that some esoteric writers at this day continue to regard ancient Greece and Rome as centres of alchemical knowledge. It is true that the Abbe Pernety, at the close of the last century, demonstrated to his own satisfaction that all classical mythology was but a vesture and veil of the *Magnum Opus* and the fable of the Golden Fleece is regarded as a triumphant vindication of classical wisdom in the deep things of transmutation. But this is precisely one of those airy methods of allegorical interpretation which, once fairly started, will draw the third part of the earth and sea, and the third part of the stars of heaven, in the tail of its symbolism. Neither in Egypt, in Greece, or in Rome, has any trace of Alchemy been discovered by historical research till subsequent to the dawn of the Christian era, and in the face of this fact it is useless to assert that it existed secretly in those countries, because no person is in a position to prove the point. All that is known upon the problem of the origin of Alchemy in the Western Hemisphere is to be found in Berthelot's *Collection des Anciens Alchimistes Grecs*, and the exhaustive erudition which resulted in that work is summed up in the following statement:- "Despite the universal tradition which assigns to Alchemy an Egyptian Origin, no hieroglyphic document relative to the science of transmutation has yet been discovered. The Graeco-Egyptian Alchemists are our sole source of illumination upon the science of Hermes, and that source is open to suspicion because subject to the tampering of mystic imaginations during several generations of dreamers and scholastics. In Egypt, notwithstanding, Alchemy first originated; there the dream of transmutation was first cherished;" but this was during and not before the first Christian centuries.

The earliest extant work on Alchemy which is as yet known in the West is the papyrus of Leide, which was discovered at Thebes, and is referable to the third century of this era. It contains seventy-five metallurgical formulae, for the composition of alloys, the surface coloration of metals, assaying, etc. There are also fifteen processes for the manufacture of gold and silver letters. The compilation, as Berthelot points out, is devoid of order, and is like the notebook of an artisan. It is pervaded by a spirit of perfect sincerity, despite the professional improbity of the recipes. These appear to have been collected from several sources, written or traditional. The operations include tinging into gold, gilding silver, superficial coloring of copper into gold, tincture by a process of varnishing, superficial aureation by the humid way, etc. There are many repetitions and trivial variations of the same recipes. M. Berthelot and his collaborator regard this document as conclusively demonstrating that when Alchemy began to flourish in Egypt it was the art of sophistication or adulteration of metals. The document is absolutely authentic, and "it bears witness to a science of alloys and metallic tinctures which was very skilful and very much advanced, a science which had for its object the fabrication and falsification of the matters of gold and silver. In this respect it casts new light upon the genesis of the idea of metallic conversion. Not only is the notion analagous, but the practices exposed in this papyrus are the same as those of the oldest Greek alchemists, such as pseudo-Democritus, Zosimus, Olympiodorus, and pseudo-Moses. This demonstration is of the highest importance for the study of the origins of Alchemy. It proves it to have been founded on something more than purely chimerical fancies- namely, on positive practices and actual experiences, by help of which imitations of gold and silver were fabricated. Sometimes the fabricator confined himself to the deception of the public, as with the author of Papyrus X (i.e., the Theban Papyrus of Leide), sometimes he added prayers and magical formulae to his art, and became the dupe of his own industry." Again: "The real practices and actual manipulations of the operators are made known to us by the papyrus of Leide under a form the most clear, and in accordance with the recipes of pseudo-Democritus and Olympiodorus. It contains the first form of all these procedures and doctrines. In pseudo-Democritus and still more in Zosimus (the earliest among the Greek alchemists), they are already complicated by mystical fancies; then come the commentators who have amplified still further the mystical part, obscuring or eliminating what was practical, to the exact knowledge of which they were frequently strangers. Thus, the most ancient texts are the clearest."

Now, there are many points in which the occultist would join issue with the criticism of M. Berthelot, but it is quite certain that the Egyptian papyrus is precisely what it is described to be, and there is, therefore, no doubt that the earliest work which is known to archaeology, outside China, as dealing with the supposed transmutation of metals is in reality a fraudulent business. This fact has to be faced, together with any consequences which it rigidly entails. But before concluding this paper it will be well to notice (I.) That it is impossible to separate the Leide papyrus from a close relationship with its context of other papyri; as admitted by Berthelot, who says:- "The history of Magic and of Gnosticism is closely bound up with that of the origin of Alchemy, and the alchemical papyrus of Leide connects in every respect with two in the same series which are solely magical and Gnostic." (II.) That, as Berthelot also admits, or, more correctly, as it follows from his admissions, the mystic element entered very early into alchemical literature, and was introduced by persons who had no interest in the practical part, who therefore made use of the early practical documents for their own purposes. (III.) That the Leide papyrus can scarcely be regarded as alchemical in the sense that Geber, Lully, Arnold, Sendivogius, and Philalethes are alchemical writers. It neither is nor pretends to be more than a thesaurus of processes for the falsification and spurious imitation of the precious metals. It has no connection, remote or approximate with their transmutation, and it is devoid of all alchemical terminology. In itself it neither proves nor disproves anything. If we can trace its recipes in avowedly alchemical writers, as M. Berthelot declares is the case, then, and then only, it may be necessary to include alchemists in the category of the compiler of this papyrus.

PART THREE

THE next stage of inquiry into the validity of the venous answers which have been given to this question will take us by an easy transition from the nature of the Leide papyrus to that of the Byzantine collection of ancient Greek alchemists. It will he recollected from last month that the processes contained in the papyrus are supposed to represent the oldest extant form of the processes tabulated by Zosinius, psendo-Democritus, and others of the Greek school. The claims of this school now demand some brief consideration for the ultimate settlement of one chief point, namely, whether they are to be regarded as alchemists in the sense that attaches to the term when it is applied as advigoration of men like Arnold, Lully, and Schmurath. It was stated last month that the compiler of the Leide papyrus could not be so regarded, and it will, furthermore, pass without possible challenge that no person could accuse that document of any spiritual significance. The abbreviated formulae of a common medical prescription are as likely to contain the secret of the tincture or the mystery of the unpronounceable tetrad. In proceeding to an appreciation of the Greek alchemists, our authority will he again M. Berthelot, who offers a signal and, indeed, most illustrious instance of the invariable manner in which a genuine and unbiased archeologist who is in no sense a mystic can assist a mystic inquiry by his researches. M. Berthelot offers further a very special example of unwearied desire after accuracy, which is not at all common even among French savants, and is quite absent from the literary instinct of that nation as a whole. The fullest confidence may always be reposed in his facts.

The collection of Greek alchemists, as it now exists, was formed during the eighth or ninth century of the Christian era, at Constantinople. Its authors are cited, says Berthelot, by the Arabian writers as the source of their knowledge, and in this manner they are really the fountain-head of Western alchemy as it is found during the middle ages, because the matter was derived from Arabia. The texts admit of being separated into two chief classes, of which one is historical and theoretical, the other technical and covered with special fabrications, as for example, various kinds of glass and artificial gems.

It is outside the purpose of an elementary inquiry to enumerate the manuscript codices which were collated for the publication of the text as it was issued by M. Berthelot in 1847. It is sufficient to say that while it does not claim to include the whole of the best alchemists, it omits an author who was judged to be of value either to science or archeology, and it is thus practically exhaustive. The following synthetic tabulation will be ample for the present purpose: – a. General Indications, including a *Lexicon of the best Chrysopeia*, a variety of fragmentary treatises, an instruction of Iris to Honris, &c.   b. Treatises attributed to Democritus or belonging to the Democritic school, including one addressed to Dioscorus by Sycresius, and another of considerable length by Olympiodorus the Alexandrian philosopher. c. The works of Zosinius the Panopolite. d. A collection of ancient authors, but in this case the attribution is frequently apocryphal, and the writings in some instances are referable even to so late a period as the fifteenth century. Pelopis the philosopher, Ortanes, Iamthichers, Agathodamion and Moses are included in this section. e. Technical treatises on the goldsmith's art, the tincture of copper with gold, the manufacture of various glasses, the sophistic coloring of precious stones, fabrication of silver, incombustible nelphom, &c. f. Selections from technical and mystical commentators on the Greek alchemists, including Stephanus, the Christian philosopher, and the Anonymous Philosopher. This section is exceedingly incomplete, but M. Berthelot is essentially a scientist, and from the scientific standpoint the commentators are of minor importance.

The bulk of these documents represent alchemy as it was prior to the Arabian period according to its ancient remains outside Chinese antiquities, and any person who is acquainted with the Hermetic authors of the middle ages who wrote in Latin, or, otherwise, in the vernacular of their country, will most assuredly find in all of them the source of their knowledge, their method, and the terminology of the Latin adepts. For, on examination, the Greek alchemists are not of the same character as the compiler of the Leyden papyrus, though he also wrote in Greek. With the one as with the other the subject is a secret science, a sublime gnosis, the possessor of which is to be regarded as a sovereign master. With the one as with the other it is a divine and sacred art, which is only to be communicated to the worthy, for it participates in the divine power, succeeds only by divine assistance, and invokes a special triumph over matter. The love of

God and man, temperance, unselfishness, truthfulness, hatred of all imposture, and the essential preliminary requlsites which are laid down most closely by both schools. By each indifferently a knowledge of the art is attributed to Hermes, Plato, Aristotle, and other great names of antiquity, and Egypt is regarded as *par excellence* the country of the great work. The similarity in each instance of the true process is made evident many times and special stress is laid upon a moderate and continuous heat as approved to a violent fire. The materials are also the same, but in this connection it is only necessary to speak of the importance attributed to many of the great alchemists in order to place a student of the later literature in possession of a key to the correspondence which exist under this head. Finally, as regards terminology, the Greek texts abound with references to the egg of the philosophers, the philosophical stone, the same which is not a stone, the blessed water, projection, the time of the work, the matter of the work, the body of Morpresia, and other arbitrary names which make up the bizarre company of the mediaeval adepts. This fact therefore must be faced in the present enquiry, and again with all its consequences: that the Greek alchemists so far as can be gathered from their names were alchemists in the true sense of Lully and Arnold: that if Lully and Arnold are entitled to be regarded as adepts of a physical science and not as physical chemists, then Zosinius also is entitled to he so regarded: that if Zosinius and his school were, however, houseminters of metal, it is fair to conclude that men of later generations belong to the same category: that, finally, if the Greek alchemists under the cover of a secret and pretended sacred science were in reality fabricators of false sophisticated gold and riches, there is at any rate one presumption that those who reproduced their terminology in like manner followed their objects, and that the science of alchemy ended as it begun, an imposture, which at the same time may have been in many cases "tempered with superstition", for it is not uncommon to history that those who exploit credulity finish by becoming credulous themselves.

It is obvious that here is the crucial point of the whole inquiry, and it is necessary to proceed with extreme caution. M. Berthelot undertakes to show that the fraudulent recipes contained in the Leyden papyrus are met with again in the Byzantine collection, but the judgment which would seem to follow obviously from this fact is arrested by another fact which in relation to the present purpose is of very high importance, namely, that a mystic element had already been imported into alchemy, and that some of those writers who reproduce the mystic processes were not chemists and had no interest in chemistry. Now, on the assumption that alchemy was a great spiritual science, it is quite certain that it veiled itself in the chemistry of its period, and in this case does not stand or fall by the quality of that chemistry, which, as M. Berthelot suggests, may very well have been only imperfectly understood by the mystics who, on such a hypothesis, undertook to adopt it. The mystic side of Greek alchemical literature will, however, be dealt with later on.

PART FOUR

WHEN the transcendental interpretation of alchemical literature was first enunciated, the Leyden papyruses had indeed been unrolled, but they had not been published, and so also the Greek literature of transmutation, unprinted and untranslated, was only available to specialists. This same interpretation belongs to a period when it was very generally supposed that Greece and Egypt were sanctuaries of chemical as well as transcendental wisdom. In a word, the origins of alchemy were unknown except by legend. Now this paper has already established the character of the Leyden papyrus numbered X. in the series, and it was seen that there was nothing transcendental about it. On the other hand, it was also stated that the Byzantine collection of Greek alchemists uses the same language, much of the same symbolism, and methods that are identical with those of the mediaeval Latin adepts, whose writings are the material on which the transcendental hypothesis of alchemy has been exclusively based, plus whatsoever may be literally genuine in the so-called Latin translations of Arabian writers. Does the Byzantine collection tolerate the transcendental hypothesis? Let it be regarded by itself for a moment, putting aside on the one hand what it borrowed from those sources of which the Leyden Papyrus is a survival, and on the other what it lent to the long line of literature which came after it. Let it be taken consecutively as it is found in the most precious publication of Berthelot. There is a dedication which exalts the sovereign matter, and seems almost to deify those who are acquainted therewith; obviously a spiritual interpretation might be placed upon it; obviously, also, that interpretation might be quite erroneous. It is followed by an alphabetical *Lexicon of Chrysopeia*, which explains the sense of the symbolical and technical terms made use of in the general text. Those explanations are simply chemical. The Seed of Venus is verdegris; Dew, which is a favorite symbol with all alchemists, is explained to be mercury extracted from arsenic, *i.e.*, sublimed arsenic; the Sacred Stone is chrysolite, though it is also the Concealed Mystery; Magnesia, that great secret of all Hermetic philosophy, is defined as white lead, pyrites, crude vinegar, and female antimony, *i.e.*, native sulphur of antimony. The list might be cited indefinitely, but it would be to no purpose here. The Lexicon is followed by a variety of short fragmented treatises in which all sorts of substances that are well known to chemists, besides many which cannot now be certainly identified, are mentioned; here again there is much which might be interpreted mystically, and yet such a construction may be only the pardonable misreading of unintelligible documents. In the copious annotations appended to these texts by M. Berthelot, the allusions are, of course, read chemically. Even amidst the mystical profundities of the address of *Isis to Horis*, he distinguishes allusions to recondite processes of physical transmutation. About the fragments on the Fabrication of Asem and of Cinnabar, and many others, there is no doubt of their chemical purpose. Among the more extended treatises, that which is attributed to Democritus, concerning things natural and mystic, seems also unmistakably chemical; although it does term the tincture, the Medicine of the Soul and the deliverance from all evil, there is no great accent of the transcendental. As much may be affirmed of the discourse addressed to Leucippus, under the same pseudonymous attribution. The epistle of Synesius to Dioscorus, which is a commentary on pseudo-Democritus, or, rather, a preamble thereto, exalts that mythical personage, but offers no mystical interpretation of the writings it pretends to explain. On the other hand, it must be frankly admitted the treatise of Olympiodorus contains material which would be as valuable to the transcendental hypothesis as anything that has been cited from mediaeval writers- for example, that the ancient philosophers applied philosophy to art *by the way of science* – that Zosinius, the crown of philosophers, preaches union with the Divine, and the contemptuous rejection of matter- that what is stated concerning minera is an allegory, for the philosophers are concerned not with minera but with substance. Yet passages like these must be read with their context, and the context is against the hypothesis. The secret of the Sacred Art, of the Royal Art, is literally explained to be the King's secret, the command of material wealth, and it was secret because it was unbecoming that any except monarchs and priests should be acquainted with it. The philosopher Zosinius, who is exalted by Olympiodorus, clothes much of his instructions in symbolic visions, and the extensive fragments which remain of him are specially rich in that bizarre terminology which characterized the later adepts, while he discusses the same questions which most exercised them, as, for example, the time of the work. He is neither less nor more transcendental than are these others. He speaks often in language mysterious and exalted upon things which are capable of being understood spiritually, but he speaks also of innumerable material substances, and of the methods of chemically operating thereon. In one place he explicitly distinguishes that there are two sciences and two wisdoms, of which one is concerned with the purification of the soul, and the other with the purification of copper into gold. The fragments on furnaces and other appliances seem final as regards the material object of the art in its practical application. The writers who follow Zosinius in the collection, give much the same result. Pelagus uses no expressions capable of transcendental interpretation. Ostanes gives the quantities and names the materials which are supposed to enter into the composition of the all-important Divine Water. Agathodaimon has also technical recipes, and so of the rest, including the processes of the so-called Iamblichus, and the chemical treatise which, by a still more extraordinary attribution, is referred to Moses. The extended fragments on purely practical matters, such as the metallurgy of gold, the tincture of Persian copper, the coloring of precious stones, do not need investigation for the purposes of a spiritual hypothesis, their fraudulent nature being sufficiently transparent, despite their invoking the intervention of the grace of God.

There is one other matter upon which it is needful to insist here. The priceless manuscripts upon which M. Berthelot's collection is based contain illustrations of the chemical vessels employed in the processes which are detailed in the text, and these vessels are the early and rude form of some which are still in use. This is a point to be marked, as it seems to point to the conclusion that the investigation of even merely material substances inevitably had a mystic aspect to the minds which pursued them in the infancy of physical science.

PART FIVE

The next point in our inquiry takes us still under the admirable auspices of M. Berthelot, to the early Syriac and the early Arabian alchemists. Not until last year was it possible for anyone unacquainted with Oriental languages to have recourse to these storehouses, and hence it is to be again noted that the transcendental interpretation of Alchemy, historically speaking, seems to have begun at the wrong end. In the attempt to explain a cryptic literature it seems obviously needful to start with its first developments. Now, the Byzantine tradition of Alchemy came down, as it has been seen, to the Latin writers of the middle ages, but the Latin writers did not derive it immediately from the Greek adepts. On the contrary, it was derived to them immediately through the Syriac and Arabian Alchemists. What are the special characteristics of these till now unknown personages? Do they seem to have operated transcendentally or physically, or to have recognized both modes? These points will be briefly cleared up in the present article, but in the first place it is needful to mention that although the evidence collected by Berthelot she's that Syria and Arabia mediated in the transmission of the Hermetic Mystery to the middle age of Europe, they did not alone mediate. "Latin Alchemy has other foundations even more direct, though till now unappreciated... The processes and even the ideas of the ancient Alchemists passed from the Greeks to the Latins, before the time of the Roman Empire, and, up to a certain point, were preserved through the barbarism of the first mediaeval centuries by means of the technical traditions of the arts and crafts." The existence of a purely transcendental application of Alchemical symbolism is evidently neither known nor dreamed by M.Berthelot, and it will be readily seen that the possibility of a technical tradition which reappears in the Latin literature offers at first sight a most serious and seemingly insuperable objection to that application. At the same time the evidence for this fact cannot be really impugned. The glass-makers, the metallurgists, the potters, the dyers, the painters, the jewellers, and the goldsmiths, from the days of the Roman Empire, and throughout the Carlovingian period, and still onward were the preservers of this ancient technical tradition. Unless these crafts had perished this was obviously and necessarily the case. To what extent it was really and integrally connected with the mystical tradition of Latin Alchemical literature is, however, another question. The proofs positive in the matter are contained in certain ancient technical Latin Treatises, such as the *Compositiones ad Tingenda, Mappa Clavicula, De Artibus Romanorum, Schedula diversarum Artium, Liber diversarum Artium,* and some others. These are not Alchemical writings; they connect with the Leyden papyrus rather than with the Byzantine collection; and they were actually the craft-manuals of their period. Some of them deal largely in the falsification of the precious metals.

The mystical tradition of Alchemy, as already indicated, had to pass through a Syriac and Arabian channel before it came down to Arnold, Lully, and the other mediaeval adepts. Here it is needful to distinguish that the Syriac Alchemists derived their science directly from the Greek authors, and the Arabians from the Syriac Alchemists. The Syriac literature belongs in part to a period which was inspired philosophically and scientifically by the School of Alexandria, and in part to a later period when it passed under Arabian influence. They comprise nine books translated from the Greek Pseudo-Democritus and a tenth of later date but belonging to the same school, the text being accompanied by figures of the vessels used in the processes. These nine books are all practical recipes absolutely unsuggestive of any transcendental possibility, though a certain purity of body and a certain piety of mind are considered needful to their success. They comprise further very copious extracts from Zosimus the Panopolite, which are also bare practical recipes, together with a few mystical and magical fragments in a condition too mutilated for satisfactory criticism. The extensive Arabic treatise which completes the Syriac cycle, is written in Syriac characters, and connects closely with the former and also with the Arabian series. It is of later date, and is an ill-digested compilation from a variety of sources. It is essentially practical.

The Arabian treatises included in M. Berthelot's collection contain *The Book of Crates, The Book of El-Habib, The Book of Ortanes,* and the genuine works of Geber. With regard to the last the students of Alchemy in England will learn with astonishment that the works which have been attributed for so many centuries to this philosopher, which are quoted as of the highest authority by all later writers, are simply forgeries. M. Berthelot has for the first time translated the true Geber into a Western tongue. Now all these Arabic treatises differ generally from the Syriac cycle; they are verbose, these are terse; they are grandiose, these are simple; they are romantic and visionary, these are unadorned recipes. The book of El-Habib is to a certain extent an exception, but the Arabian Geber is more mysterious than his Latin prototype. El-Habib quotes largely from Greek sources, Geber only occasionally but largely from treatises of his own, and it is significant that in his case M. Berthelot makes no annotations explaining, whether tentatively or not, the chemical significance of the text. As a fact, the Arabian Djarber, otherwise Geber, would make a tolerable point of departure for the transcendental hypothesis, supposing it to be really tenable in the case of the Latin adepts.

Preceding papers have taken the course of inquiry through the Greek, Arabian, and Syrian literatures, and the subject has been brought down to the verge of the period when Latin alchemy began to flourish. Now before touching briefly upon this which is the domain of the spiritual interpretation, it is desirable to look round and to ascertain, if possible, whether there is any country outside Greece and Egypt, to which alchemy can be traced. It must be remembered that the appeal of Latin alchemy is to Arabia, while that of Arabia is to Greece, and that of Greece to Egypt. But upon the subject of the *Magnum Opus* the Sphinx utters nothing, and in the absence of all evidence beyond that of tradition it is open to us to look elsewhere. Now, it should be borne in mind that the first centre of Greek alchemy was Alexandria, and that the first period was in and about the third century of the Christian era. Writing long ago in *La Revue Theasophique*, concerning *Alchemy in the Nineteenth Century*, the late Madame Blavatsky observes that "ancient China, no less than ancient Egypt, claims to be the land of the alchemists and of physical and transcendental alchemy; and China may very probably be right. A missionary, an old resident of Pelun, William A. P. Martin, calls it the 'cradle of alchemy.' Cradle is hardly the right word perhaps, but it is certain that the celestial empire has the right to class herself amongst the very oldest schools of occult science. In any case alchemy has penetrated into Europe from China as we shall prove." Madame Blavatsky proceeded at some length to "compare the Chinese system with that which is called Hermetic Science," her authority being Mr. Martin, and her one reference being to a work entitled *Studies of Alchemy in China* by that gentleman.

When the present writer came across these statements and this reference, he regarded them as an unexpected source of possible light, and at once made inquiry after the book cited by Madame Blavatsky, but no person, no bibliography, and no museum catalogue could give any information concerning a treatise entitled *Studies of Alchemy in China,* so that these papers had perforce to be held over pending the result of still further researches after the missing volume. Mr. Carrington Bolton's monumental *Bibliography of Chemistry* was again and again consulted, but while it was clear on the one hand that Mr. Martin was not himself a myth, it seemed probable, as time went on, that a mythical treatise had been attributed to him. Finally, when all resources had failed, and again in an unexpected manner, the mystery was resolved, and Mr. W. Emmett Coleman will no doubt be pleased to learn – if he be not aware of it already – that here as in so many instances which he has been at the pains to trace, Madame Blavatsky seems to have derived her authority second-hand. The work which she quoted was not, as she evidently thought, a book separately published, but is an article in *The China Review,* published at Hong Kong. From this article Madame Blavatsky has borrowed her information almost verbatim, and indeed where she has varied from the original, it has been to introduce statements which are not in accordance with Mr. Martin's, and would have been obviously rejected by him.

Mr. Martin states (I) that the study of alchemy "did not make its appearance in Europe until it had been in full vigor in China for at least six centuries, or *circa* B.C. 300. (2) That it entered Europe by way of Byzantium and Alexandria, the chief points of intercourse between East and West. Concerning the first point Madame Blavatsky, on an authority which she vaguely terms history, converts the six centuries before A.D. 300, with which Mr. Martin is contented, into sixteen centuries before the Christian era, and with regard to the second she reproduces his point literally. Indeed, it is very curious to see how her article, which does not treat in the smallest possible degree of alchemy in the nineteenth century, is almost entirely made up by the expansion of hints and references in the little treatise of the missionary, even in those parts where China is not concerned. Mr. Martin, himself more honorable, acknowledges a predecessor in opinion, and observes that the Rev. Dr. Edkins, some twenty years previously, was the first, as he believes to "suggest a Chinese origin for the alchemy of Europe." Mr. Martin, and still less Dr. Edluns, knew nothing of the Byzantine collection, and could not profit by the subsequent labors of

M. Berthelot, and yet it is exceedingly curious to note that the researches of the French savant do in no sense explode the hypothesis of the Chinese origin of alchemy, or rather, for once in a season to be in agreement with Madame Blavatsky, perhaps not the origin so much as a strong, directing, and possibly changing influence. The Greek alchemists appeal, it is true, to Egypt, but, as already seen, there is no answer from the ancient Nile, and China at precisely the right moment comes to fill up the vacant place.

The mere fact that alchemy was studied in China has not much force in itself, but Mr. Martin exhibits a most extraordinary similarity between the theorems and the literature of the subject in the far East and in the West, and in the course of his citations there are many points which he himself has passed over, which will, however, appeal strongly to the Hermetic student. There is first of all, the fundamental doctrine that the genesis of metals is to be accounted for upon a seminal principle. Secondly, there is the not less important doctrine that there abides in every object an active principle whereby it may attain to "a condition of higher development and greater efficiency." Thirdly, there is the fact that alchemy in China as in the West was an occult science, that it was perpetuated "mainly by means of oral tradition," and that in order to preserve its secrets a figurative phraseology was adopted. In the fourth place, it was closely bound up with astrology and magic. Fifthly, the transmutation of metals was indissolubly allied to an elixir of life. Sixthly, the secret of gold-making was inferior to the other arcanum. Seventhly, success in operation and research depended to a large extent on the self-culture and self-discipline of the alchemist. Eighthly, the metals were regarded as composite. Ninthly, the materials were indicated under precisely the same names: lead, mercury, cinnabar, sulphur, these were the chief substances, and here there is no need to direct the attention of the student to the role which the same things played in Western alchemy. Tenthly, there are strong and unmistakable points of resemblance in the barbarous terminology common to both literatures, for example, "the radical principle," "the green dragon," the "true lead," the "true mercury," etc.

In such an inquiry as the present everything depends upon the antiquity of the literature. Mr. Carrington Bolton includes in his bibliography certain Chinese works dealing with Alchemy, and referred to the third century. Mr. Martin, on the other had, derives his citations from various dates, and from some authors to whom a date cannot be certainly assigned. Now, he tells us, without noticing the pregnant character of the remark, that "one of the most renowned seats of Alchemic industry was Bagdad, while it was the seat of the Caliphate" – that an extensive commerce was "carried on between Arabia and China" – that "in the eighth century embassies were interchanged between the Caliphs and the Emperors" – and, finally, that "colonies of Arabs were established in the seaports of the Empire." As we know indisputably that Arabia received Alchemy from Greece, it is quite possible that she communicated her knowledge to China, and therefore, while freely granting that China possessed an independent and ancient school, we must look with suspicion upon its literature subsequent to the eighth century because an Arabian influence was possible. But, independently of questions of date, comparative antiquity, and primal source, the chief question for the present purpose is whether Chinese Alchemy was spiritual, physical, or both. Mr. Martin tells us that there were two processes, the one inward and spiritual, the other outward and material. There were two elixirs, the greater and the less. The alchemist of China was, moreover, usually a religious ascetic. The operator of the spiritual process was apparently translated to the heaven of the greater genii. As to this spiritual process Mr. Martin is not very clear, and leaves us uncertain whether it produced a spiritual result or the perpetuation of physical life.

The Great Symbols
Of The Tarot

ON the hypothesis that there is or may be a deeper meaning in the chief Tarot Symbols than attaches thereto on the surface, it becomes necessary to establish certain preliminary points as an initial clearance of issues, and I will premise in the first place that by chief Symbols I mean those only which I have been in the habit of denominating Trumps Major in other writings on the subject. First among the preliminary points there is the simple fact that we know nothing certainly concerning the origin of Tarot cards. As usual, however, in matters belonging to occult arts and so-called science, the place of knowledge has been occupied by uncritical reveries and invention which is not less fraudulent because the fraud may be frequently unconscious. When the artist Gringonneur, in or about the year 1393, is affirmed to have produced a set of picture-cards for the amusement of King Charles VI of France, it has been affirmed that some of their designs were identical with Tarot Trumps Major. The evidence is the fact of certain beautiful and antique card-specimens – in all about twenty-six – which are scattered through different continental muse-ums and were attributed in the past to Gringonneur. They are now held to be of Italian origin, more or less in the early years of the fif-teenth century, and there are no extant examples prior to that period. But to establish this point on expert authority at its value is not to fix the origin of Tarot cards in respect of date or place. It is idle, I mean, to affirm that Venetian, Bolognese and Florentine vestiges of sets al-located to 1400-1418 are the first that were ever designed. In view, however, of the generations of nonsense which we have heard testi-fying on the subject; it must be said that it is equally idle and more mischievous to affirm that they are not. When, towards the close of the eighteenth century, Court de Gebelin first drew attention, as a man of learning and an antiquary, to the fact of Tarot cards, he pro-duced sketches of the Trumps Major in the eighth volume of Le Monde Primitif. In the form that he had met with they were not priceless works of art like those in the Bibliotheque Nationale, but rough, primi-tive and barbarous, or precisely of that kind which might be expected to circulate in country places, among lower classes of players and gamblers, or among gypsies for purposes of fortune-telling. Suppos-ing that they had been designed and invented originally about the period mentioned, nearly four centuries had elapsed, which were more than ample time for them to get into general circulation throughout the countries in which they were traced by Court de Gebelin- namely, Southern France, Spain, Italy and Germany. If the Trumps Major were originally distinct from the minor emblems, there was also full op-portunity for them to be joined together. But alternatively the designs, perhaps even in several styles, may have been old already in the year 1400- I am speaking of the Trumps Major- in which case they were married much later to the fifteenth century prototypes of our modern playing-cards. It will be seen that the field is open, but that no one is entitled in reason to maintain either view unless evidence should be found to warrant it in the designs themselves, apart from the real or presumptive age of the oldest extant copies.

Having done something in this summary manner to define the historical position, the next point is to estimate the validity of those speculations to which I have referred already. It is not possible on this occasion, nor do I find that it would serve a purpose, to do more than recapitulate my own previous decisions, readied as the result of researches made prior to 1910. The first and most favored hypothesis concerning Tarot cards is that they are of Egyptian origin, and it was put forward by him who to all intents and purposes may be called their discoverer, namely, Court de Gebelin. It has been set aside long since by authorities apart from predispositions and ulterior purposes in view. De Gebelin was an Egyptologist of his day, when Egyptology was in its cradle, if indeed it can be said to have been born, and that which he did was to excogitate impressions and formulate them in terms of certitude. They have not been borne out, and their doom from the standpoint of sane scholarship may be said to have been sealed when they fell into the hands of French occult dreamers and were espoused zealously by them. The most salient and amazing elaborations were those of Eliphas Levi in 1856 and onward. The designs were for him not only Egyptian in the sense of the earliest dynasties, but referable to the mythical Hermes and to the prediluvian wisdom of Enoch. They formed otherwise the traditional Book of Adam which was brought to him in Paradise by an angel, was removed from him at the Fall, but was restored subsequently in response to his earnest supplications. Eliphas Levi did more, however, than theorize on the subject. He gave pictorial illustrations of the cards restored to their proper primeval forms, in which they appeared as pseudo-Egyptian designs, the work of an amateur hand. The same practice prevailed after Levi had ceased to publish. It was developed further by Christian, while long after him, under the auspices of Oswald Wirth and others, the Trumps Major appear in all the panoply of imitative Delta art. These things are to all intents and purposes of dishonest device, but very characteristic unfortunately after their own manner, for the marriage of speculative occultism and intellectual sincerity has hardly ever been made in France and seldom enough elsewhere.

These are the preliminary points which are placed here for consideration – as I have said, to clear the issues. In the complete absence of all evidence on the subject, we must be content to carry an open mind as to where the Tarot originated, remembering that the earliest designs with which we are acquainted do not connote antiquity, unless possibly in one case, and unless the early fifteenth century may be regarded as old enough in the absence of a *partis-pris*. The statement obtains also respecting cards of any kind, including the Baldini emblems, which are neither Tarots nor counters for divination, or games of chance.

I satisfied myself some years ago, and do not stand alone, that the Trumps Major existed originally independently of the other arcana and that they were combined for gambling purposes at a date which it is possible to fix roughly. I am concerned only on the present occasion with what may be called the Great Symbols. They are twenty-two in number, and there is no doubt that some of them correspond to estates and types. The Emperor and Empress, the Pope and Juggler belong obviously to this order, hut if we put them back speculatively even to medieval times we cannot account in this manner for the so-called Pope Joan or High Priestess. She must be allocated to another sequence of conditions, under another scheme of human community at large. It is to be noted that though Venetian, Florentine, and French packs differ somewhat clearly, between narrow limits of course, Pope Joan has never been termed the Abbess in any, nor can I recall that she has been so depicted that such a denomination could apply and thus include the design among ecclesiastical estates in Christendom. She comes, therefore, as I have intimated, from another region and another order of things. This is the one Tarot Trump Major which suggests a derivation from antiquity, not however in the sense of Court de Gebelin, who referred it to Isis, but to an obscure perpetuation of pagan faith and rite in Italy which the inquiries of Leland seem to have established as a matter of fact. In this case, and at the value of his researches, on which I have commented elsewhere, Pope Joan represents not improbably a vestige of the old Astarte cultus. I do not pretend to be satisfied with the explanation, but it may be accepted tentatively perhaps and does not necessarily carry the question of antiquity behind mediaeval times. In the midst of all the obscurity, one only point emerges in all certainty: whatever the card may have stood for originally, it was not the mythical female pope, an ascription which arose as a leap in the dark of ignorance on the part of people – whether in France or Italy – who knew the Pope Joan legend but had never heard of Astarte and much less of Isis. I should regard it as a rather old leap.

I have spoken of classification under types, estates or classes, but it obtains only in respect of a few designs, seeing that the majority of the Trumps Major are occasionally allegorical and in several cases can be understood only as belonging to a world of symbols, while a few are doctrinal in character- in the sense of crude Christian doctrine. The Resurrection card and the Devil belong to this last class.

Death, on the other hand, is a very simple allegorical picture-emblem, like the Lovers, Justice and Strength. The symbolical cards, which must be so termed because certainly they do not correspond to the admitted notions of allegory, are the Hanged Man, Chariot, the so-called card of Temperance, the Tower, the Star, the Sun and Moon, and that which passes under several names, one of which is the World. The Wheel of Fortune is seemingly of composite character, partaking of both allegory and symbolism, while the Fool is very difficult to class. On the surface he may be referable to that estate which inhabits the lowlife deeps- the mendicant and vagabond type. He suggests the Italian lazzaroni, except that he carries a wallet, as if he were on his way through the world. He recalls, therefore, the indescribable rabble which followed the armies in crusading and later times. He is the antithesis of the Juggler, who flourishes at the expense of others by following a knavish trade, or who profits alternatively by the lower kind of skill.

When Court de Gebelin described the Trumps Major in connection with the rest of the Tarot pack, he gave an account of their use in games of hazard, but he had heard also of their divinatory value and was at some pains to ascertain the process by which they were adapted to this purpose, in which way he is our first authority for the traditional meanings of the cards as counters in the telling of fortune. He represents in this manner another landmark in the obscure history of the subject. It is to be assumed that his knowledge was confined to the practice in France, and there are no means of knowing whether Spain, Italy and Germany followed other methods at that time. I believe that Alliette or Etteilla varied the divinatory meanings on the threshold of the nineteenth century in accordance with his own predilections, as he altered the Trumps Major themselves in respect of their arrangement and changed the original names in certain cases. In the year 1856, as we have seen, Eliphas Levi began to issue his occult revelations, based largely on the Trumps Major, developing their philosophical meanings in a most elaborate manner. They are at times exceedingly suggestive and always curious, but it must be understood that in occult matters he depended solely on personal intuitions and invention. There was a time, over twenty years since, when I was led to think otherwise, in view of evidence which has proved worthless on further and fuller investigation. Levi said on his own part that he owed his "initiation" only to God and his personal researches, but some of his French admirers have not hesitated, this notwithstanding, to affirm his direct connection with Masonic Rites and Orders. The question does not signify, for initiations of this kind would not have communicated occult knowledge. It follows that his Tarot System – if such it can be called – is at best a work of ingenuity but often a medley of notions, and it owes, so far as can be ascertained, nothing whatever to the past which extends behind Court de Gebelin. The point is not without importance, because he speaks with an accent of great authority and certitude when P. Christian went still further in *L'homme rouge des Tuileries* and in his *Histoire de la Magie*, the same criticism applies, as there is no need to say that it does in the labored excogitations of Papus, Stanislas de Guaita, and others of the French school.

Now, there are twenty-two Trumps Major arranged, more or less in a sequence but subject to certain variations as the packs differ respecting time and place of origin. There are also twenty-two letters of the Hebrew alphabet, and it occurred to Eliphas Levi that it was desirable to effect a marriage between the letters and cards. It seems impossible to make a combination of this kind, however arbitrary, and not find some accidents in its favor, and there is better authority in Kabalism than Eliphas Levi ever produced in writing to connect the Hebrew letter Beth with the so-called Pope Joan or Sovereign Priestess of the Tarot. But he was concerned very little with any root in analogy, or he might have redistributed the Trumps Major, seeing that their sequence is – as I have said – subject to variation in different sets and that there seems no particular reason to suppose that any arrangement of the past had a conscious purpose in view. In this manner he might have found some curious points by taking the old Yetziratic classification of the Hebrew letters and placing those cards against them which corresponded to their conventional allocations. It was sufficient, however, for his purpose that there are twenty-two letters and twenty-two palmary symbols, and if he remembered, he cared nothing apparently for the fact that the numerical significance of Hebrew letters belies his artificial combination after the letter Yod. We can say if we choose that the eleventh Trump is that which is called Strength, though it depends on the arrangement adopted in the particular pack; but the letter Caph is not eleven in the alphabet, for it corresponds to the number 20. Death is the thirteenth card and seems placed well in the Tarot sequence because thirteen is the number of mortality; but the letter Nun is 40 and has no such fatal connection. The folly of the whole comparison is best illustrated by the card which is called the Fool and is not numbered in the series, the cipher Nought being usually placed against it. In Levi's arrangement it corresponds to the letter Shin, the number of which is 300. But wherever it is placed in the series the correspondence between Trumps Major and the Hebrew alphabet is ipso facto destroyed.

It is to be noticed further that Levi allocated meanings to each letter individually of the Hebrew alphabet, but they are his own irresponsible invention, except in two or three very obvious cases – e.g., that Beth, the second letter, corresponds to the duad, Ghimel to the triad, and Daleth to the tetrad. It may be interesting to note that his number 15, which answers to the Tarot symbol of the Devil, is explained to be so-called occult science, an eloquent tribute to his own fantastic claims in respect of the subject which he followed. As an explanation unawares it is otherwise of some value, for there is of course no ordered occult science, though there are certain forms of practice which bring into operation those psychic powers of which we know darkly in the way of their manifestation only, and it is a matter of experience that they are more likely to open the abyss rather than the Path to Heaven.

Levi's instituted connection between Tarot cards and the Hebrew alphabet has proved convincing to later occultism in France and elsewhere. He is also the originator of another scheme which creates a correspondence of an equally artificial kind between the four suits, namely, Clubs, Cups, Swords and Pantacles; which make up the Lesser Arcana of the Tarot, and the Ten Sephiroth of Kabalistic theosophy. Because of the number four it was inevitable that in a mind like his they should be referred to the four letters of the Sacred Tetragram – Jod, He, Vau, He – which are commonly pronounced Jehovah. It is the uttermost fantasy as usual, as exhibited by his attempted identification of Jod with Clubs, while Cups and Pantacles or Deniers are both coerced into correspondence with the letter He. As regards the constituent cards of the four suits, even his ingenuity failed to discover a ground of comparison between the Sephiroth and the Court-cards, so he offers the following couplet as a commentary on the King, Queen, Knight and Knave or Squire:

The married pair, the youth, the child, the race:
Thy path by these to unity retrace.

But this comes to nothing, for the Knight is not necessarily a youth, nor does the ancient or modern Jack correspond to the idea of a child. Had Levi understood Sephirotic Kabalism better, again he could have done better by affirming – as it would have been easy for him – that the French *damoiseau* had replaced a primitive *damoislle*, the Squire Court-card being really feminine. He could then have allocated correctly as follows: the King to Chokmah, the Queen to Binah, the Knight to the six lower Sephiroth from Chesed to Yesod inclusive, governed by the semi-Sephira Daath, and the damoiselle to Malkuth. He would have found also this manner a complete correspondence between these Trumps Minor and the four letters of the Tetragram. Finally, he would have established the operation of the Sacred Name in the four Kabalistic worlds and would have exhibited the distinctions and analogies between Shekinah in transcendence and the Shekinah manifested in life and time. But Levi was the magus of a world of fancy and not of a world of knowledge.

He found his opportunity, however, with the so-called pips, points or numbered cards, for he had the clear and talismanic fact that there are ten numbered cards in each suit, while the Sephiroth are also ten. But because there is no other correspondence in the nature of things he did badly enough in the development and produced the following nonsense rhymes, which are borrowed from the literal translation that I have made elsewhere.

Four signs present the Name of every name.
Four brilliant beams adorn His crown of flame.
Four rivers ever from His wisdom flow.
Four proofs of His intelligence we know.
Four benefactions from His mercy come.
Four times four sins avenged His justice sum.
Four rays unclouded make His beauty known.
Four times His conquest shall in song be shown.
Four times He triumphs on the timeless plane.
Foundations four His great white throne maintain.
One fourfold kingdom owns His endless sway,
As from His crown there streams a fourfold ray.

In this manner the four Aces correspond to Kether because it is the first Sephira in the mystery of coming forth from Ain Soph Aour, the Limitless Light; the four twos to Chokmah, four threes to Binah and so forward till the denary is completed. But what is to be understood by the four proofs of Divine Understanding, the four Divine Benefactions and the sixteen sins which are avenged by Geburah or Justice we know as little as of the reason for believing that the Divine Victories shall be celebrated only four times in song, or how in the philosophy of things it is possible to triumph four times on a plane where no time exists. If Eliphas Levi could have furnished the omitted explanations, it is certain that Zoharic Kabalism knows nothing about them.

At the back of all these reveries is the well-known fact that the ten Sephiroth are inter-connected in the Kabalistic Tree of Life by means of twenty-two paths, to which the Hebrew letters are attributed, Kether communicating with Chokmah by the Path of Aleph, with Binah by that of Beth, and so downward. A diagram showing these allocations was published by Athanasius Kircher in Oedipus Oegyptiacus. The allocation of the Tarot Trumps Major to the Paths of the Tree of Life is obviously the next step, and attempts have been made in this direction by blundering symbolists, but they have forgotten that in the Mystical Tree the Sephiroth are also Paths, making thirty-two Paths of Wisdom, from which it follows that in the logic of things there ought to be thirty-two Trumps.

The study of the Tarot has been pursued since the days of Levi in France, England and America, the developments being sometimes along lines established by him and sometimes the result of an independent departure. Speaking generally, he has been followed more or less. I have shown that his allocations are for the most part without any roots in the real things of analogy, while as to later students of the subject all that they have to offer is ingenuities of their own excogitation. We have to recognize, in a word, that there is no canon of authority in the interpretation of Tarot symbolism. The field is open therefore: it is indeed so open that any one of my readers is free to produce an entirely new explanation, making no appeal to past speculations: but the adventure will be at his and her own risk and peril as to whether they can make it work and thus produce a harmony of interpretation throughout. The sentence to be pronounced on previous attempts is either that they do not work, because of their false analogies, or that the scheme of evolved significance is of no real consequence. There is an explanation of the Trumps Major which obtains throughout the whole series and belongs to the highest order of spiritual truth: it is not occult but mystical; it is not of public communication and belongs to its own Sanctuary. I can say only concerning it that some of the symbols have suffered a pregnant change. Here is the only answer to the question whether there is a deeper meaning in the Trumps Major than is found on their surface.

And this leads up to my final point. If anyone feels drawn in these days to the consideration of Tarot symbolism they will do well to select the Trumps Major produced under my supervision by Miss Pamela Coleman Smith. I am at liberty to mention these as I have no interest in their sale. If they seek to place upon each individually the highest meaning that may dawn upon them in a mood of reflection, then to combine the messages, modifying their formulation until the whole series moves together in harmony, the result may be something of living value to themselves and therefore true for them.

It should be understood in conclusion that I have been dealing with pictured images; but the way of the mystics ultimately leaves behind it the figured representations of the mind, for it is behind the kaleidoscope of external things that the still light shines in and from within the mind, in that state of pure being which is the life of the soul in God.

The Book of the Secret Word
and the Higher Way to Fortune

IT is difficult to offer a comprehensive handbook of divination, fortune-telling and the connected curious arts without making at least some reference in passing to the so-called Book of Thoth which has been accepted by numerous authorities as the most richly productive mode for the automatic induction of prophetic insight that has been transmitted from the past. As it is impossible, however, in the present place to do the first thing which is essential in respect of the subject – that is, to provide the cards themselves[1] – I propose only to say a few words concerning them and the use to which they can be put from a new point of view. It must be explained in the first place that Tarot cards are the precursors of our ordinary playing-cards and that a complete pack contains 78 symbols or talismanic and hieroglyphic pictures, as follows

A. 22 Special Trump Cards, which have no analogy with anything in their extant descendants.

B. 5 ordinary Court Cards in each of the four Suits, and these are: Ace, King, Queen, Prince or Knight, and Novice, Page or Squire.

C. The small Cards of the 4 Suits, numbered – by the fact of their Symbols – 2 to 10, it being understood that the Suits are Cups, replacing Hearts; Swords, corresponding to Spades; Wands, substituted for Diamonds; and Pantacles, representing Clubs.

All the cards indifferently are covered with hieroglyphics or signs, following particular laws of sequence and connected intimately with the mysteries of occult science and philosophy. The use of the cards is (1) for playing in the ordinary sense at a game of skill and hazard – but it should be added that as a mere diversion they have long since passed out of vogue; (2) for the usual art of fortune-telling in its several varieties, a particular method being occasioned by the multiplicity of the elements; (3) for those other practices which are included by the term Divination; and (4) for the higher uses of the imagination in the mystic oracles of the soul. In this department the true mode of their application is reserved by certain sanctuaries of adeptship; and if for the purposes of the present review it were assumed that I – whose identity has been concealed for many years of occult life under the name of Grand Orient – hold any place or office in these Secret Temples, it must be obvious that I could not – supposing that I had even the wish – betray their mysteries. But as one who has followed in many departments of research the science of the soul and her different paths of light, I have found other mysteries which can be attached to the Tarot cards, and these – if they are followed faithfully – will open many secrets to those who have the needful gifts of intuition, or sight within.

The student must, in the first place, set aside all that has been said upon the archaeology of the Book of Thoth; it does not signify for our purpose whether the cards are very ancient – though this they are undoubtedly – or whether they are an invention of yesterday. It does not matter whether they originated in Egypt or much further East. In fine, all published philosophical and practical explanations as to their scope or application must be set out of court entirely, without prejudice to their value within measures for other purposes, though it should be stated that no one has been in a position to tell the truth concerning them.

I must assume now that the cards are in the possession of my reader, for they can be obtained by those who seek[2] In commencing his operation he will separate the 22 Trump Cards from those of the Four Suits, and after this sifting he will further extract the card which is numbered Nothing in the Trump Series and which bears the title of THE FOOL. Despite the miserable appearance and name of this symbolic figure, the student must understand that this is a very important card. It signifies in a triple sense: (a) The wisdom of this world, which is foolishness with God; (b) the folly of the Cross; and (c) the uninitiated person, which – as we shall find in the sequel – can be understood after two manners. In accordance with these three meanings there are as many primary operations possible: (1) concerning matters of worldly prudence; (2) concerning the life of devotion in the things of religion, but understood rather conventionally – that is to say, ancient, accepted and orthodox, with a tendency towards the formal side; (3) concerning the soul's progress towards the term of its research. Now, it must be understood that it is not lawful to make the same demand a second time in the first series till, by the event declaring itself up to a certain point, there has been a new situation created and therefore a new warrant for such enlightenment. To do otherwise would invite that which is understood by fatality, or at least make void all element of true foresight in both operations.

The demand may be regarding the operator himself or a Querent who is seeking knowledge at his hands. In either case indifferently, he is represented by the Fool, the reason being that in respect of the inquiry he is in a state of ignorance.

As we are not dealing with elements of common fortune-telling, our next task is to ascertain the limits of the three worlds of inquiry. In matters of ordinary human prudence, it is assumed that the Querent is in a state of doubt and solicitude concerning some question of grave importance by which the course of his material life is likely to be affected. He is not seeking information on his chances at the next lottery or the winning horse at an immediately forthcoming race. The life of devotion is more especially allocated to cases of conscience, and it should be understood that the oracle, for example, reveals nothing on new matters of doctrine. It does not solve doubts concerning the Trinity or explain mysteries of eschatology – except indeed indirectly, by counsel, interpretation, and turning the intention of the seeker towards those holy things in which doubt and difficulty dissolve. On the other hand, the soul's progress is concerned with the highest spiritual things, and these are exclusive to the third world of research. The answer in all cases is found by the dealing of the Trump Cards in direct relation to the Prime Card of the Fool in the particular matters, and the process shows the evolution of that symbolic personality from a state of darkness and ignorance to one of light and understanding concerning it. Before any attempt at working, the Querent and the Operator, if two persons are concerned, or otherwise the Querent who operates on his own account, should spend a certain time in recollection and silent prayer for guidance. As no special form is necessary, none will be given here; it is the contemplation and prayer of the soul. The 21 Trump Cards, are then shuffled and dealt, but what follows is an experience of the intuitive faculty, the gift of inward sight, and the interpretation of signs which possess a wealth of meaning.

It is because the whole experiment constitutes an experiment in intuition and not a counsel of adeptship that, although the cards may be arranged after several manners, I have adopted the most simple mode. They could be grouped, for example, about the central figure, which is that of the Querent, but this would involve a particular distribution of the symbolism belonging to a higher grade of the whole experiment. I say therefore that the Cipher Card being placed on one side, to stand throughout for the Querent, the 21 Trumps must be dealt after shuffling in a single line, and from the place of the various symbols contained therein, they are constructed by the gift of the operator into an intelligible revelation according to the testimony of the arrangement thus fortuitously secured and according to the plane of the question. It will serve no purpose to limit the range of the symbols in the three worlds, and I will give therefore seven typical examples allocated to each; but in the first place I will enumerate the mystic titles attributed to the cards themselves: –

1. The Juggler.
2. High Priestess.
3. Empress.
4. Emperor.
5. Pope, or Hierophant.
6. Lovers.
7. Chariot.
8. Justice.
9. Hermit.
10. Wheel of Fortune.

11. Fortitude, or Strength.
12. Hanged Man.
13. Death.
14. Temperance.
15. Devil, or Typhon.
16. Ruined Tower.
17. Star.
18. Moon.
19. Sun.
20. The Last Judgment.
21. The World.
22 = 0. The Fool.

It should be understood that the long sequence of lesser cards does not enter into the scheme of the present operation, not that they are beside its issues, but because they would involve the statement of certain facts in occult divination which have never been made public, while if I furnished some idle substitute it would tend to the deception of the student, with whom I am seeking here to deal in all sincerity.

There follows thus and now the signification of the Trump Cards in the three worlds of research.

I. WORLD OF HUMAN PRUDENCE

1. The Juggler – Skill in any department within the sphere of the subject; subtlety; savoir faire; on the evil side, trickery; also occult practice, apart from the wisdom of adeptship.

2. High Priestess – Nature generally and particularly also as regards her operations, including therefore the material side of generation and reproduction; fertility; change.

3. Empress – The sphere of action; the feminine side of power, rule and authority; woman's influence; physical beauty; woman's reign; also the joy of life, and excesses on the evil side.

4. Emperor – Logical understanding, experience, human wisdom; material power on the male side, and all involved thereby.

5. Pope, or Hierophant – Aspiration, life, power of the keys; spiritual authority developed on the external side; temporal power of official religion; on the evil side, sacerdotal tyranny and interference.

6. Lovers – Material union, affection, desire, natural love, passion, harmony of things; contains also the notions of modus vivendi, concord and so forth; equilibrium.

7. Chariot – Triumph of reason; success in natural things; the right prevailing; also predominance, conquest, and all external correspondences of these.

8. Justice – Equilibrium on the mental side rather than the sensuous, for which see No.6; under certain circumstances, law and its decisions; also occult science.

9. Hermit – Caution, safety, protection; wisdom on the manifest side; and the isolation thereof; detachment; the way of prudence; sagacity; search after truth.

10. Wheel of Fortune – Mutation, circumstances; revolution of things, vicissitude; time and its variable development; all that is understood by the external side of fortune.

11. Fortitude, or Strength – Courage, vitality, tenacity of things, high endurance.

12. Hanged Man – The symbol of renunciation, for whatever cause and with whatever motive.

13. Death – Contains naturally the meaning implied by its name and illustrated by its pictorial symbol, but not only and not at all of necessity; transforming force, independent of human will; may signify destruction; power behind the world which alters the face of the world, but it is this power in one of its respects only.

14. Temperance – New blood, combination, admixture, with the object of amelioration; providence in desirable change.

15. Devil, or Typhon – Fatality, evil, the false spirit; can indicate also the good working through evil.

16. Ruined Tower – Destruction, confusion, judgment; also the idea of Divine Wrath.

17. Star – Light descending, hope; the symbol of immortality.

18. Moon – Half-light, mutation, intellectual uncertainty, region of illusion; false-seeming.

19. Sun – Full light, intellectual and material; the card of earthly happiness, but not attained individually.

20. The Last Judgment – Resurrection; summons to new things; a change in the face of everything.

21. The World – The glory thereof under the powers of the higher providence, the sum of manifest things; conclusion on any subject.

II. WORLD OF CONFORMITY

1. The Juggler – The official side in religion, but containing the warrants thereof; also the arbitrary, mechanical side, and formalism.

2. The High Priestess – The Church as an organism; the growth of the man therein; Church doctrine.

3. The Empress – The sphere of Church action on the spiritual side; also desire and its wings; spiritual principle.

4. The Emperor – Executive power of religion; its work in realization upon man; active mind of the Church; the Church as a power in the world and in the life of the individual.

5. The Pope – Doctrine, and especially its admitted and orthodox side; the agreement of minds in faith; the teaching power.

6. Lovers – Love of religion, union therewith, but on the external side; marriage of the Church and the natural heart; the power which draws from natural things; also grace which makes for conversion, but is not conversion itself.

7. Chariot – Reason exalted in religion; victory of the moral faculties; apotheosis of the logical understanding in faith; first conquest of the natural man.

8. Justice – The power which makes the best of both worlds; middle path; lesser salvation; balance between good and evil; goodness, but not raised above the sphere of temptation.

9. Hermit – Asceticism, denial, detachment; the state attained by these; but also a light which enlighteneth; one who has isolated himself that in fine he may lead others; the principle which all this signifies.

10. Wheel of Fortune – The sword and the crown; another symbol of equilibrium, in this case over the mutations of fortune; the angel of true life, the spirit of religion ruling over the flux of circumstance.

11. Fortitude, or Strength – The conquest of Nature by those who can say with their heart and their will: *Esto mihi turris fortitudinis*; the soul overcoming.

12. Hanged Man – Crucifixion and self-crucifixion; atonement.

13. Death – Mortal sin; resurrection to the life of Grace, as an antitype - depending on the environment of the card.

14. Temperance – The principle of sacramental life; the mixture of things Divine with things human, for the transmutation of the lat-

ter; the increase which Grace gives; in fine, this card is a Symbol of the Eucharist, the entrance of the Divine into the nature of man.

15. Devil, or Typhon – Rebellion; the spirit which denies; especially, false doctrine, which is the worship of Satan.

16. Ruined Tower – The Fall, and here especially the fall from Grace; also judgment on sin; the ruin of the house of life, when evil has prevailed therein; but the symbolism is that of a Divine act or consequence, and the power which destroys the Temple of God can rebuild it in three mystical days.

17. Star – Holy works – spiritual and corporal – poured upon the earth of humanity; also the gifts of the Spirit poured upon the earth of the individual; the soul manifesting by works.

18. Moon – Sufficing Grace; the soul mourning over the sadness of material life and the lapse into matter.

19. Sun – Lord of Glory; efficacious grace; spiritual joy; the life of holiness poured over the life of man.

20. The Last Judgment – Separation of good from evil; summons to ascend; examination of conscience; resurrection in the soul.

21. The World – The Law and State of Paradise; Shekinah; Divine Presence; the soul in the condition of attainment; end of religion in the individual, but this is not to be understood as Divine Union; it is more properly the state of Grace.

III. WORLD OF ATTAINMENT

1. The Juggler – That which must be overcome; the will in this connection; the motive of this world.

2. The High Priestess – Divine intuition; the holy soul, having the book of the Mysteries opened, and reading therein; the first form of personal illumination.

3. The Empress – Higher soul of man; woman clothed with the sun; she who is born of aspiration, who comes in the signs of power and perfect rule; the soul that has attained wings.

4. The Emperor – Lord on the higher planes; the fulfillment of the Great Work of spiritual adeptship; the victory over all things.

5. Pope, or Hierophant – The life which leads to the Doctrine; the power which leads the individual into all truth; the priesthood that is within.

6. Lovers – Spiritual marriage; the union of man with his soul; the state of conversion.

7. Chariot – The triune man, having consciousness in his three worlds; the living symbol of the invisible God; he that overcometh.

8. Justice – Higher grades of the narrow path; equilibrium on the spiritual side; greater salvation; the perfect life.

9. Hermit – The secrets of the King; Divine Science; the light of the world within.

10. Wheel of Fortune – Divine rapture; triumph over the circle of necessity; in this world, the wheel has ceased to revolve.

11. Strength – The will to go forward; the world overcome; the fortitude of those who are established in God.

12. Hanged Man – The path of choice; reversion of the natural man; he who has not loved his life even to the loss thereof; conquest of the fear of those who can kill the body.

13. Death – Mystical death; the price of immortality; that which is entered with the will that there may be life evermore.

14. Temperance – Emergence of the consciousness; realization of the Divine Immanence; super-added Grace.

15. Death or Typhon – The last enemy; the demon of spiritual pride; the abyss opening; the spirit of Antichrist.

16. Ruined Tower – The rending of the House of Doctrine in the heart of the individual; final impenitence.

17. The Star – Life of life; descent of the Divine; waters of life freely.

18. Moon – Spiritual fantasy.

19. Sun – Plenary consciousness in God; the Spirit rules; God encompassing; Orient from on high.

20. Judgment – The state of one who says: Behold, I come quickly – that is, in answer to the call from the heights; resurrection in the complete man.

21. The World – Unveiled mystery; term of research; redeemed Nature; Divine Consciousness; the Beatific Vision.

As regards the Fool, this card, which has been sufficiently explained already, signifies the consummation of everything, when that which began his initiation at zero attains the term of all numeration and all existence. The card which bears no number passes through all the numbered cards and is changed in each, as the natural man passes through worlds of lesser experience, worlds of devotion, worlds of successive attainment, and receives the everlasting wisdom as the gift of perseverance.

It is further to be understood that the significance of all the cards in each of the three worlds is modified by the cards in their immediate vicinity, and this to such an extent that the present section of the Manual might be increased into a large volume if an attempt were made to expose even the major variations. It is not to be expected therefore that the operator will read correctly from the beginning, since he is learning a new alphabet, and its combinations exceed calculation. He must attain familiarity by practice; he must have also the second sight of the mind – the power of discerning analogies and distinctions in the midst of analogies. I now proceed to give a few specimen questions belonging to each of the series, after which I shall reach a conclusion of the matter for the present purpose by three constructions of the sense attributable to three assumed distributions of the Trump Cards, as the result of a hypothetical dealing.

WORLD OF HUMAN PRUDENCE

1. What will be the consequence on my life of a marriage which I now contemplate – it being understood that I am not actuated simply by personal attraction, or solely by physical desire?

2. My affairs have passed into disorder, and finding that my fortune is imperiled on the material plane, after what manner shall I try to meet the difficulty?

3. What must I do to ensure success in life and the improvement of my worldly position, having full regard to my moral and spiritual duties?

4. Is it desirable to embrace the opportunity which offers for my removal into a foreign country?

5. The world is wide before me, and the best years of my life: what light can I obtain on the question of vocation or business?

6. What course shall I pursue in the serious emergency which has arisen?

7. Shall I have the necessary health and strength to pursue those projects which have become so important in my life?

WORLD OF CONFORMITY

1. I am troubled about questions of doctrine and desire light thereon: in what direction shall I look?

2. I am in a state of serious temptation – in what shall I find help to withstand?

3. My sins have found me out: what course shall I pursue?

4. I have resolved upon a better life: to what means of grace shall I have recourse above others?

5. I am in the state that is called by spiritual writers one of drought and dryness: how can I find consolation?

6. Shall I improve my chances of salvation by a change in my external religion?

7. I feel a certain vocation towards the ministry, and I desire light on the subject.

WORLD OF ATTAINMENT

1. What is, literally speaking, that kind of life which does lead to the Doctrine, and what form of it applies to my individual case?

2. I am conscious of substantial increase in intellectual light upon spiritual mysteries, but not of increase in holiness. What shall I do?

3. Wherein lies the path of rebirth?

4. What must I do to attain eternal life?

5. How shall I exchange the disposition towards spiritual things for their real experience?

6. In what does the Beatific Vision consist?

7. What is the great secret of the Inward Life?

It should be laid to heart, firstly, that these specimen questions do not exhaust the possible subjects of research, which are indeed innumerable: they are cited only to show the things that belong to the three several worlds. Secondly, it should be understood – at least as regards the Worlds of Conformity and Attainment – that it would be an act of sacrilege to ask from curiosity, or as if to test the powers of an oracle. This is no question of ordinary Divination, but of a prayerful search after light on the things that concern the soul, and it is to the higher soul within us that we must look for the answer. When the Aspirant has become familiar by practice with the inexhaustible deeps of enlightenment which lie imbedded in the Tarot Cards, he will find that a triple answer is possible to every question – that is to say, in its relation to each of the three worlds of mystical philosophy. So elaborate a quest must not be attempted in the present instance, but only a guide in outline for purposes of study. The threefold meanings attributed to each of the cards are the key of the whole process, and any operation is not an inquiry into future chances or an attempt to unveil futurity, on however high a plane, but is the analogical and mystical explanation of the law which inheres in the symbols, however combined.

The first hypothetical case will be taken from The World of Human Prudence. Question 7: A young man inquires what light he can obtain as to his future course in this world. The results of the dealing are 3, 4, 1, 17, 9, 14, 12, 15, 16, 8, 13, 10, 11, 19, 2, 5, 6, 7, 21, 20, 18. The cards 11 and 18 are upside down, reducing that which is good and accentuating that which is evil. It will be seen that the cards work out very curiously, with the predominance of woman's influence (3) at the beginning, and change (20) in the face of everything having the term of the whole subject (21) on its left, while the latter has success and triumph. But the card which precedes this final triplicity is that of marriage. The object being therefore to know the Querent's future course, it is clear that his welfare depends on a material union. The first triplicity shows that his own powers have, as predominating factors, his own skill on one side and the feminine side of power on the other. His hope (17) has all his tact (1) on the left and the safety of caution (9) on the right, indicating that to attain his end subtlety and savoir faire must be checked by prudence. Reasonable unselfishness (12) is threatened by the evil and false spirit (15), but it has combination (14) suggested by the idea of marriage on the other side, so that his saving will be in the altruism of his union with a woman. That equilibrium which is the desirable path of life (8) is threatened by destruction (16) and by the symbol of death (13). It is a very bad combination, and he must seek to unite himself with the transforming force which is independent of human will (13 alternatively) – otherwise, with the law of the universe. Unfortunately, his courage (11) is reversed, with vicissitude on the one side, though earthly happiness is signified on the other. I gather that he has one way of escape in the consolations of official religion (5), which again has a marriage card (2) on its left, namely, fertility, and marriage itself on the right It is no happy outlook unless there is happiness in his marriage, which is not the subject of inquiry. It is in any case by marriage that he must begin.

The World of Conformity – Question 7: The Aspirant feels a certain vocation towards the ministry and desires light on the subject. The results of the dealing are 5, 6, 15, 10, 14, 4, 7, 16, 12, 1, 18, 3, 9, 8,

20, 21, 19, 17, 11, 13, 2. Card 11 is reversed. The first card which comes out (5) is that of doctrine on the orthodox side and of the teaching power. The second is that of the love of religion, of marriage between the heart and the Church (6). With these on the one side and the ruling spirit of religion on the other (10), the tendency to false doctrine (15) is held in check, and the man will be a safe teacher, one who may administer the sacraments efficaciously (14), one possessing the capacity to influence his fellow-man for good (4). The chances of fall from Grace (16) are counterbalanced by reason exalted in religion (7); but this depends upon crucifixion of self (12), and this in turn can check formalism in religion (1), while such formalism is balanced on the other side by Grace (18), coming from communion with the Church. Goodness (8) has detachment (9) on the one side and spiritual rebirth (20) on the other, showing plainly how natural virtue is exalted into the supernatural. The end of research (21), being the question put, but also life in Grace, has the summons to ascend (20) and Efficacious Grace (19) on either hand, the result of which is the life of holiness. Good works (17) come before and can be made to overrule what is lacked in strength (11 reversed), and if the latter card shows that the Querent is by no means outside the sphere of temptation, he has the Church (2) to aid him and to change sin (13) into resurrection into new life and Grace. In fine, the cards, which begin in doctrine and end in the ecclesiastical assembly, show throughout that the Aspirant is meant for the ministry.

World of Attainment – Question 1: What is the kind of life which leads to the doctrine? The results of the dealing are 11, 19, 18, 15, 3, 5, 17, 13, 9, 8, 16, 10, 7, 6, 2, 20, 4, 21, 14, 1, 12. Card 20 is reversed. In the search after attainment in the soul, the sequence of the symbols begins with the will to go forward (11) and concludes with the path of choice (12) in the conquest of the natural man. Between these two lies the sum of all perfection. The end is Divine Consciousness (21), which is the life of knowledge. It has the victory over all things (4) on the one side and realization of the Divine Immanence (14) on the other. The dawning of the Orient from on high (19) is beheld on entering the path, and this rules on the one side over (18) spiritual fantasy, while the ruling of the spirit (19) is well placed between fantasy (18), which it suffuses, and the conquest of the world (11). Spiritual pride and the spirit of Antichrist (15) have, it is true, the symbol of illusion on the one side, but the higher soul of man (3) is on the other. It is clear, however, that the last enemy is also a very strong one. The life which leads to the Doctrine (5) is between the ascent of the soul (3) and the life of life (17). It is on the ascent of the one that the other comes down, namely, the Divine, and the union of the two is that life which does lead to the real knowledge. Mystical death (13) is overshadowed on the one side by Divine Grace communicated (17) and on the other by Divine Science (9). The possibility of fall from righteousness (16) is checked by perfect life (8) and the rapture of aspiration towards the Divine (10). The three-fold nature of man (7) has that aspiration (10) on the one hand and on the other its end, which is the mystical marriage of God and man (6). In this connection the card (20) of rebirth reversed, having the Holy Soul (2) and the victory over all things (4) on either side, must be taken to mean rather that it is judgment against the soul which is reversed, if the man follows the path. That which must be overcome (1) stands between superadded grace (14) and the sign of him (12) who has not loved his life to the loss thereof. I say therefore that the sequence of cards has indeed set forth the kind of life which not only leads to the Doctrine but to the whole term of spiritual knowledge.

And these are the first indications to those who can see concerning the Book of Thoth, which I have called the Way to Fortune.

Notes:

1. The version of 1912 adds ", which should be obtained separately".

2. The footnote to the 1909 edition reads, "The prices of complete Tarot packs may be obtained on application to the publishers of this Manual.", while the footnote to the 1912 edition (subsequent to the publishing of the Waite-Smith deck) reads, "The Key to the Tarot, together with a complete pack of cards, may be obtained on application to the publishers of this Manual."

Touchstone

THE destiny of Faerie is a gilt-edged security for those who are faithful and true. After days and weeks and months of quest and venture, I was licensed to look into the Law of Fate in Faerie and to learn how it is consulted by means of a Dial of Flowers. The inward working of spells is made known thereby, but the way out of them is not declared. I learned it in another place and long after: it is one of the secret laws. You follow the course of destiny in Faerie, as you do on this earth of ours but it is thus only till you have learned to distentangle its skein. It is then in your hands, and- if you are wise- it can be woven at your own will so that the Law follows you thenceforward. For destiny is consequence, and that upon which it is consequent is we ourselves alone. So it is true that the Book of Fate in Faerie is the Book of the Art of its Ruling.

There was a Prince who had lost his history through the service of a spell, so that no name is given him. It is needful, on occasion, to be lost before you can find your way; but when I met with him in

Faerie, I did not know without seeking whether that which had bechanced him was of evil, which passes, or of hidden goodness, unfolding like a flower from within. He had no memory of his birth-place, his forbears and heritage, or aught of his opening life. A mourn-ful gift of divination was mine in Faerie, and the same is a gift of second sight. Now, there is a certain bond of concord between these kinds of workings and the fall of the evening dew, for which reason I made use of my oracles under the first star. I consulted my Book of Fate, the reading of which is like the sleep of beauty and of magic. I must not tell you my method; but I found that the Prince was heir to a throne in the Kingdom over the way, and he had great treasures in birthright. He was the descendant of a faerie race, full of powers and privileges. Over his cradle the Houses of Heaven – which are twelve – shone as new houses in a renewed heaven, looking as if over a vir-gin earth. Yet was he deprived of his history, but wit you well, it was because of great things which might be fulfilled concerning him. As to these I did not see in my glass. I had awakened in Faerie and was learned in mysteries of silken couches, of tapestried rooms and lad-ders of golden rope, of secret keys, of ivory gates and the paths that lead therefrom. I knew also of a certain mysterious repose in Faerie, when the powers of enchantment soften and Nature moves in her sleep. In this manner I had one key of enchantment, but of the way out of all enchantments – which goes due east and explains them all as you go – I had learned nothing as yet.

So further concerning this Prince: he was brought from a far and blessed country, to be abandoned in the dark labyrinth of a forest, which is more full of glamour and misdirection than is a picture of painted images. Like a child made by magic, he discovered himself awake therein. You might judge that he was a Prince by the golden fillet on his head, and another traveller from a land that is very far away – having been once in like case – uncovered the misfortune that had come over the high Prince by means of the heart's remembrance and obvious tests. He sent him through the world in search of a sec-ond history testifying that something of his old estate should unfold in every loyal and sacred venture undertaken and carried to its term by him who was bewrayed.

I know not how long this Prince lingered over the vintages and winepress of Faerie or with maids created for joy who fool some trav-ellers therein. But he came to himself on a day and was presently in a quest of stars, which is a good beginning anywhere. A call in the heart of a star; a star which sings in its calling; the star and its call shall lead. He found some stars moreover – yes, even in the sandhills and the marshes. But they were not worlds, unhappily; and though one by one the scenes of his past came back, they were only as ghosts or dreams – like tales told in the twilight, which are not believed in day. Then he was counselled to discover the Stone called Touchstone, which opens all doors of mystery. My companion and fellow – traveller, seeking for treasure of gold, does it happen that you possess the Touchstone? Do you dream what it is, my child of wonder? It tests and tries everything, and nothing of all resists. It is like a dream which is behind dream; it leads to the Land of Reality, on God's side of the Land of Dream; it brings the good dreams true. By its aid you can find the meaning in Tales of Faerie. It comes to you on the blade of a drawn sword, and that sword is like the parting of ways for ever.

The Prince who has lost his history has been to the Valley of Vision, but the King sleeps therein. He has been to the Land of Irem, but the hidden City is still empty and desolate. He has drunk at the Fountain of Borico, where a man may find his youth, though he has left it long since at a corner of streets remote. He has knelt in the Temple of Isis, which has a girdle of mysteries and a Holy Place within it, about which the mysteries worship. He has watched in the Groves of Dodona, where the trees – which are old as the world – whisper with human voices, and he has ascended the highest peak of the Holy Mountain Kaf. He has spoken with Harut and Marut, the fallen angels who first taught magic to man. He has been to the tombs of the Magian Kings, which are watched by the Star of Bethlehem – till the second dawn of the day of Christ. He has sorrowed with Vathek and Solomon in the Hall of Eblis, wherein they suffer until their sins are whitened. He has tarried with Gian ben Gian, the King of the Pens. But he has not found that cube which is called Touchstone. Now this is great sorrow, and I have pledged myself to seek through the whole earth and the whole starry heaven for that which will open the eyes, so that even a Prince- in his passing through pageants like these- may know that it is in his heart already- that white and shining Talisman. I travel in search of this and the water of all-seeing. I am pledged to seek out the Touchstone for a Prince who has lost his history. Are you he for whom I work, tell me, or shall I look for another?

The Threefold Division of Mysticism

A magazine which has been founded to represent, and that for the first time, the whole circle of knowledge which is included under the term occult, must obviously provide at the outset a clear notion of Mysticism – what it is, and how its branches are to be tabulated. In the popular mind the conception conveyed by the word is in all respects vague and confused. It is, nevertheless, difficult at the present day to meet with any tolerably educated person, whatever his pursuit in life, who does not confess ultimately to a certain curiosity about it. Not only in professedly intellectual circles but in the commercial world, and more singularly in that of finance, in the thronged centre of the city of London, where the congestion of this money-getting age is greatest, where, as at all centres, the rush of motion is swiftest, the writer of this paper has received over and over again evidence the most indubitable that there is a spirit of inquiry abroad, and a very general sentiment of interest in places where one would have thought that it would be least expected. There may be nothing solid in this interest, or serious in that inquiry, but the feeling is there and the curiosity at least is there; both in a certain way are significant that the awakening of the new spirit has an operation far outside the circle which is its visible limit, and, considering the classes referred to, this significance is perhaps greater than is the testimony of literature at the moment and the tendency of speculative thought in precisely the same direction. The case has been cited here because it indicates the need for definition, and it leads immediately to the keynote of this paper, which is this- that however profound and abstruse in some of its branches is that which we call Mysticism, a clear elementary comprehension of what it is can be very easily established even in the most ordinary mind. There is no reason inherent in the subject for the existing uncertainty and vagueness.

Mysticism admits of being separated into three chief divisions, and these are Transcendental Science, Transcendental Philosophy, and Transcendental Religion. The term transcendental applies to anything which is outside the normal sphere of experience, whether in fact, or thought, or faith. Transcendental Science deals with the operation and effects of forces generally unknown. Transcendental Philosophy is that body of doctrine which explains the phenomenal universe in accordance with the science of its secret laws. Transcendental Religion is the application of universal law to the interior nature of man. But while these comprehensive definitions are perfectly correct and acceptable, the actual limits of Mysticism are usually somewhat narrower. The idea of Transcendental Science is generally confined to such operations of unknown law as have a direct bearing upon Transcendental Religion, and Transcendental Philosophy does not commonly concern itself with the whole economy of the universe so much as with the intimate relations subsisting between the universe and man. A definition of Mysticism, independent of its natural classifications, will illustrate this point. It has been most rightly and philosophically defined as the endeavour of the human mind to grasp the divine essence or ultimate reality of all things, and to enjoy, while in this life and in this body, the blessedness of an immediate communion with the Highest. This being the end in view, Transcendental Science consists in the knowledge of those forces, and the laws governing the same, by which the union of man with the Divine is accomplished, and Transcendental Philosophy is the wisdom which can apply these forces once their knowledge has been given. In other words, it is a practical doctrine founded upon the experience of the Mystics. So, also, Transcendental Religion is the accomplishment of the union in question. But it is proposed by THE UNKNOWN WORLD to accept everything in its broadest sense, and to treat it from that standpoint. Thus, in the matter of Transcendental Science

it will be understood that this includes the whole circle of methods and processes by which occultists in the past have made themselves acquainted with the secret forces resident in man and the universe. It is the exploration of the unknown in Nature, and it has passed; hitherto, under another term which there is no reason to conceal, notwithstanding that it has been abused and misinterpreted by its friends as well as by its enemies. This term is Magic, and it is mentioned here because one of its most illustrious exponents has given a definition concerning it which is not only admirable in itself, but exhibits it as interchangeable with the term Transcendental Science. "Magic," says Eliphas Levi, "is the traditional science of the secrets of nature, which has come down to us from the Magi." Now, this traditional science has been perpetuated in two ways- by a literature which, to a large extent, veils the secrets, and by occult assemblies and fraternities. THE UNKNOWN WORLD will successively acquaint its readers with all that is important in all branches of the literature, and with the Mysteries which underlie its symbolism. It will acquaint them as well, up to the fullest point of possibility, with the history of the secret societies in connection with Mysticism, though at the same time the writers who may be engaged upon this work will violate no confidence with which they may have been entrusted on such a subject. Transcendental Science has several broad divisions. There is, for example, Astrology, which is the appreciation of the celestial influences in their operation upon the nature and life of man. There is Esoteric Medicine, which consists in the application of occult forces to the healing of disease in man: it includes also a traditional knowledge of the medicinal properties resident in various substances which are disregarded by ordinary pharmacy. There is Alchemy, which is the subject of a special notice elsewhere in the present issue, and does not therefore require to be defined here. It is, however, one of the most important and attractive branches of occult science. There is Divination, a term which will be made use of in THE UNKNOWN WORLD to indicate all that vast variety of methods and processes by which lucidity was supposed to be operated in suitable subjects, whether in mundane matters for the discovery of things unknown to the operator and of events to come, or in matters which are extra mundane for clairvoyant communication with spirits. This last-mentioned branch of Divination is a part of what has sometimes been termed Practical Pneumatology, and for purposes of classification it must be distinguished from that department of Transcendental Science which is commonly known as Ceremonial Magic, consisting in the scrupulous fulfillment of certain archaic rites and the operation of numerous bizarre formulae, as a result of which the Magician, or Magus, was enabled; as it is claimed, to invoke angels, demons, elemental and elementary spirits, the phantasms of the dead, and the astral entities of still living beings. A certain virtue inherent in certain words and actions is supposed by Ceremonial Magic, as also a great uninvestigated power resident in the will of the Magician, but it is open to question whether the results produced were not of the clairvoyant order.

Each and all of these Transcendental Sciences are supposed to be liable to that species of abuse which is technically known as Black Magic. The celestial influences could be perverted in the malefic composition of talismans. The malpractice of Esoteric Medicine produced the Secret Science of Poisoning, and the destruction of health, reason, or life by unseen forces. The perversion of Alchemy resulted in the sophistication of metals, and on this subject there is quite an extensive literature still extant. In like manner, Divination was debased into Witchcraft, and Ceremonial Magic into dealing with devil, compacts with demons, and other forms of transcendental delusion and imposture. The actual principles which are at the basis of the Black Art, when interpreted from the standpoint of the occultist, will be explained from time to time in THE UNKNOWN WORLD, and some extremely rare rituals never before translated will be given upon the same subject. The precise bearings of Transcendental Science upon the true ends of Mysticism will also be developed, as occasion may arise, in a very full and intelligible manner.

Transcendental Philosophy

As already indicated, is the mystical explanation of the universe, on the one hand, while on the other it is an explanation of the correlation subsisting between that universe and man. Thus, it expounds the process of development which operated in the creation of the world, and it expounds also the special quality of evolution which is still proceeding in humanity. The writings attributed to Hermes Trismegistus and the extraordinary body of literature comprised in the Jewish Kabbalah are good instances of a transcendental philosophy of the cosmos. They are not the only instances which have become generally known in the West, while over and above all written record there is affirmed to be the unwritten record of esoteric investigation and experience transmitted from remote ages by the occult associations before referred to, and not beyond attainment at the present day by a properly qualified aspirant. The evidences which can be gleaned in connection with this important claim will be considered at a proper time in the pages of THE UNKNOWN WORLD. Concerning the evolution of humanity and the forces at work therein, as unfolded by mystic philosophy, it seems scarcely necessary to promise that this will have adequate treatment. It leads up to the end of all mysticism, the Divine Union, which also has already been mentioned. From the Hermetic standpoint, Man is the great subject; his origin, his nature, his potentialities, his destiny, constitute the one interest. There is nothing in Transcendental Science which is of any moment except in so far as it concerns him, and assists the mind of the philosopher to understand better what he is. If his destiny be written in the stars, then the stars are of moment, and Astrology is also of moment, but not otherwise does day speak unto day or night show knowledge to night, and there is no reason in all the starry depths except in their relation to the astronomer who gauges them, or to the babe who is affected by their influence. All that interests a man is man. It is the same through the whole gamut. There is no intrinsic importance in that which heals. The assuaging herb in itself is nothing; the man whom it salves is all; but when he is present the herb itself borrows importance from the possibility of its ministration to him, and from the application of his mind to its properties. Then even the "flower in the crannied wall" can tell us "what God and man is." The visible universe becomes intelligent in man, as man becomes intelligible in God. So, also, the modes of Divination are puerile, but there is no puerility about the sage who interprets the eternal world from the analogies of things which are seen. Thus, man is the focus of everything, towards him all forces tend, in him all interests centre; he is that point "through which the universe is continually passing." The very hierarchies of heaven are to him as nothing except in so far as there is some side in their nature which can adjust itself to man, so that it can exhibit a likeness to man, and put out a point for communication with him. It is for this reason that God Himself must become man in order that He can be understood by man, and can, in other and bolder words, be of any moment or importance to man, and it is also for this reason that the unknowable Deity of Agnostics is a more monstrous idol than is possessed by any pantheon. God is that which man is eternally knowing in himself, and that God is ever becoming man is a truth which must always be recognized by Mystics. Finally, the religion which most directly and vividly realizes that God takes flesh in man, and that man puts off flesh in God, is the nearest to the heart of Mysticism. It need not be here said that this is Christianity or that this is Buddhism, but, more simply that this is true religion. Thus Transcendental Science with man for its pivot gives us Transcendental Philosophy as a circle within its circle, while Transcendental Philosophy, in its turn, converging more upon the centre, leads us to Transcendental Religion

Now there are many definitions of religion, but there is one which includes all, just as there are many religions and one underlying all. It follows the philology of the word and exhibits it as a rebinding. There is nothing, it may be gratefully added, that is new in this definition; it is realized by many people who consciously are not Mystics, and it is intellectually understood by a still greater number who are not religious at all. The term rebinding involves the idea of some thing which has been set loose or has broken away from another thing. Here the reference is to the mind of man the individual which has been loosed from man the universal- the essential nature of man from the essential nature of God. It does not matter how or why this separation has taken place. It may be accepted that the Mystic has much to learn before he can plumb that mystery. It may be true that no written Mysticism, and no unwritten tradition of the inner orders, can expound it; but the end of all Mysticism as of all religion, is to attain that reunion. The possibility is not merely the fundamental doctrine of Transcendental Religion; it is the one doctrine; all else is a question of processes. Some of them may be better than some others, as some methods of divination produce the hypnotic state more readily than the rest. Hence the religion of the Mystics is the most simple, the most easy of popular understanding, because it is the least encumbered. Begin where one may in the universe it affirms that all roads ultimately lead to God. The path of vice will lead there though it passes through perdition by the way. Soul and body may be destroyed in hell but the spirit must return to God who gave it. But it is well, if it be possible, to save the soul alive, that Psyche may be united to Eros. There is no reason therefore why Mysticism should fail in the common understanding. It sees the end and it claims to know the way, while the direction of that way has no insuperable difficulties. It does not lie far from any man's walk in life, and it will be the chief object of THE UNKNOWN WORLD to simplify as far as possible the instructions of Transcendental Religion.

The Life of the Mystic

THERE are certain conventional terms which, on the one hand, do not accurately represent the construction placed upon them along a given line, but that construction has been accepted so long and so generally that the defect in the application may be regarded as partially effaced; and, on the other hand, there are also conventional terms between which a distinction has come into existence, although it is not justified by their primary significance. As regards the first class, the very general use of the term "occult movement" may be taken as an example. It is inexact after two manners: in involves at once too much and too little – too much, because it has served to represent a good deal that is not at all of the occult order; and too little, because a slight change in the point of view would bring within the range of its meaning many things which nobody who now uses it would think of including therein. The doings of more than one great secret political organization might, in the full sense of the words, require to be classed as part of the occult movement, though no one will need to be informed that the latter is not political; while certain events which have occurred and are occurring in the open day, and have all along challenged the verdict of public opinion, cannot strictly be included in occultism, as they betray none of its external characteristics. I refer to the phenomena of animal magnetism, hypnotism, spiritualism and all that which is included in the field of psychical research. In respect of the second class, a very clear differentiation now exists between the terms " occult" and "mystic," and it is one also which it is necessary to recognize, though, fundamentally speaking, the two words are identical, differing only in the fact that one of them is of Latin and the other of Greek origin By the occultist we have come to understand the disciple of one or all of the secret sciences; the student, that is to say, of alchemy, astrology, the forms and methods of divination, and of the mysteries which used to be included under the generic description of magic. The mystic is, at the first attempt, perhaps more difficult to describe, except in the terminology of some particular school of thought; he has no concern as such with the study of the secret sciences; he does not work on materials or investigate forces which exist outside himself; but he endeavors, by a certain training and the application of a defined rule of life to reestablish correspondence with the divine nature from which, in his belief, he originated, and to which his return is only a question of time, or what is commonly understood as evolution. The distinction between the occultist and the mystic, however much the representative of physical science at the present day might be disposed to resent the imputation, is therefore, loosely speaking, and at least from one point of view, the distinction between the man of science and the man of introspection. The statement, as we shall see, is not exhaustive, and it is not indeed descriptive. It may be said more fully, in the words of the late Edward Maitland, that the occultist is concerned with "transcendental physics, and is of the intellectual, belonging to science," while the mystic "deals with transcendental metaphysics, and is of the spiritual, belonging to religion." Expressed in modern terms, this is really the doctrine of Plotinus, which recognizes "the subsistence of another intellect, different from that which reasons, and which is denominated rational." Thus, on the one hand, there are the phenomena of the transcendental produced on the external plane, capable of verification and analysis, up to a certain point; and, on the other, there is the transcendental life. "That which is without corresponds with that which is within," says the most famous Hermetic maxim; indeed the connection suggested is almost that of the circumference with the centre ; and if there is a secret of the soul expressed by the term mysticism, the phenomena of the soul manifesting on the external plane must be regarded as important; but these are the domain of occultism. The importance must, of course, differ as the phenomena fall into higher and lower; the divinations of geomancy carry an appearance of triviality, while the design of ceremonial magic to establish communication with higher orders of extra-mundane intelligence wears a momentous aspect; but both are the exercise of seership, and this gift, as a testimony of the soul and her powers, is never trivial.

Assuming therefore a relationship subsisting between occult practice and the transcendental life of the soul, it seems worth while to contrast for a moment the work of the mystic with that of the disciple of occult science, so as to realize as accurately as possible the points of correspondence and distinction between Ruysbroeck, St. John of the Cross and Saint Martin, as types of the mystic school, and Arnoldus de Villanova and Martines de Pasqually, as representing the school of occult science. The examples of such a contrast must naturally be sought in the past, because, although occult science is pursued at the present day, and by some ardently, it can scarcely be said to have votaries like those who were of old. The inquiry belongs also to the past in respect of the mystic, for, to speak plainly, the saint belongs to the past. So far as the life of the outside world is concerned, there is little opportunity amidst mundane distractions for the whole-hearted labors of the other centuries. The desire of the house is indeed among us, but the zeal of it is scarcely here, not, at least, in the sense of the past.

The distinction in question is more than that which is made between the man of action and the man of reflection; it is not that which we have come to regard as differentiating the man of science from the philosopher. There are many instances of synthetic occult philosophers – among them Cornelius Agrippa and Robert Fludd – who neither divined nor evoked – who were not alchemists, astrologers or theurgists – but rather interpreters and harmonizers; and yet these men were not mystics in the proper sense of the term. Nor is the distinction quite that which constitutes the essential difference between the saint and the specialist, though the occult student of the past was in most cases a specialist who was faithful to his particular branch. The activity and the strenuousness of the life was often greater with the mystic than in the case of the man who was dedicated to some particular division of occult knowledge, though alchemist and astrologer were both laborious men – men whose patience imbued them with something of the spirit which governs modern scientific research. The ground of the contrast is in the purpose which actuated the two schools of experience. The crucible in which metals are transmuted, on the assumption of alchemy, is still a crucible and the converted metal is still a metal; so also the astrologer may trace the occult and imponderable influences of the stars, but the stars are material bodies. The practical work of the mystic concerned, on the contrary, the soul's union with God, for, to state it briefly, this, and this only, is the end of mysticism. It is no study of psychic forces, nor, except incidentally, is it the story of the soul and her development, such as would be involved in the doctrine of reincarnation. It is essentially a religious experiment and is the one ultimate and real experiment designed by true religion. It is for this reason that in citing examples of mystics, I have chosen two men who were eminent for sanctity in the annals of the Christian Church, for we are concerned only with the West; while the third, though technically out of sympathy, essentially belonged to the Church. I must not, therefore, shrink from saying that the alternative name of the mystic is that of the saint when he has attained the end of his experiment. There are also other terms by which we may describe the occultist, but they refer to the science which he followed.

The life of the mystic was then in a peculiar sense the life of sanctity. It was not, of course, his exclusive vocation; if we are to accept the occult sciences at their own valuation, more than one of them exacted, and that not merely by implication, something more than the God-fearing, clean-living spirit, which is so desirable even in the ordinary business man. He who was in search of transmutation was counselled, in the first instance, to convert himself, and the device on the wall of his laboratory was Labora but also Ora. The astrologer, who calculated the influences of the stars on man, was taught that, in the last resource, there was a law of grace by which the stars were ruled. Even the conventional magician, he who called and controlled spirits, knew that the first condition of success in his curious art was to be superior to the weakness of the inconstant creatures whose dwelling is amidst the flux of the elements.

I have said that, in most cases, the occult student was, after his manner, a specialist – he was devoted to his particular branch. Deep down in the heart of the alchemist there may have been frequently the belief that certain times and seasons were more favorable than others for his work, and that the concealed materials which he thought of symbolically as the Sun and Moon, as Mercury, Venus or Mars, were not wholly independent of star and planet in the sky; and hence no doubt he knew enough of elementary astrology to avoid afflicted aspects and malign influences. But, outside this, the alchemist was not an astrologer, and to be wise in the lore of the stars was an ambition that was sufficient for one life, without meddling in the experiments of alchemy. On the other hand, the mystic, in common with all the members of his community, having only one object in view, and one method of pursuing it – by the inward way of contemplation – had nothing to differentiate and could not therefore specialize.

Again, occult science justifies itself as the transmission of a secret knowledge from the past, and the books which represent the several branches of this knowledge bear upon them the outward marks that they are among the modes of this transmission, without which it is certain that there would be no secret sciences. The occult student was, therefore, an initiate in the conventional sense of the term – he was taught, even in astrology. There were schools of kabalism, schools of alchemy, schools of magic, in which the mystery of certain knowledge was imparted from adept to neophyte, from master to pupil. It is over this question of corporate union that we have at once an analogy and a distinction between the mystic and the occultist. The former, as we find him in the West, may in a sense be called an initiate because he was trained in the rule of the Church; but the historical traces of secret association for mystic objects during the Christian centuries are very slight, whereas the traces of occult association are exceedingly strong. The mysteries of pre-Christian times were no doubt schools of mystic experience. Plato and Plotinus were assuredly mystics who were initiated in these schools. Unfortunately the nature of this experience has come down to us, for the most part, in a fragmentary and veiled manner. But, outside exoteric writings, it has in my belief come down, and it is possible to reconstruct it, at least intellectually and speculatively, for it is embedded in the symbolic modes of advancement practised by certain secret societies which now exist among us. A transmission of mystic knowledge has therefore taken place from the past, but the evidence is of an exceedingly complex nature and cannot be explained here. Nor is it necessary to our purpose, for western mysticism is almost exclusively the gift of the Church to the West, and the experiment of Christian mysticism, without any veils or evasions, is written at large in the literature of the Church. It may call to be re-expressed for our present requirements in less restricted language, but there is not really any need to go further. "The Ascent of Mount Carmel," "The Adornment of the Spiritual Marriage," and "The Castle of the Inward Man," contain the root-matter of the whole process. I have also found it well and exhaustively described in obscure little French books which might appear at first sight to be simply devotional manuals for the use of schools and seminaries. I have found it in books equally obscure which a few decades ago would have been termed Protestant. There is the same independent unanimity of experience and purpose through all which the alchemists have claimed for their own literature, and I have no personal doubt that the true mystics of all times and countries constitute an unincorporated fellowship communicating continually together in the higher consciousness. They do not differ essentially in the East or the West, in Plotinis or in Gratry.

In its elementary presentation, the life of the mystic consists primarily in the detachment of the will from its normal condition of immersion in material things and in its redirection towards the goodwill which abides at the centre. This centre, according to the mystics, is everywhere and is hence, in a certain sense, to be found in all; but it is sought most readily, by contemplation, as at the centre of the man himself, and this is the quest and finding of the soul. If there is not an open door – an entrance to the closed palace – within us, we are never likely to find it without us. The rest of the experiences are those of the life of sanctity leading to such a ground of divine union as is possible to humanity in this life.

In the distinction – analogical, as already said – which I have here sought to establish, there lies the true way to study the lives of the mystics and of those who graduated in the schools of occult science. The object of that study, and of all commentary arising out of such lives, is to lead those, and there are thousands, who are so constituted as to desire the light of mysticism, to an intellectual realization of that light. The life of the mystic belongs to the divine degree, and it would be difficult to say that it is attainable in the life of the world; but some of its joys and consolations – as indeed its trials and searchings – are not outside our daily ways. Apart from all the heroisms, and in the outer courts only of the greater ecstasies, there are many who would set their face towards Jerusalem if their feet were put upon the way – and would thus turn again home.

The Tarot and
Secret Tradition

THE Tarot is a puzzle for archaeology and it is also an intellectual puzzle. When the bare fact of its existence first became public in Europe, the seventy-eight cards were in use as a game and also as a method of divination and may have served these purposes for generations. Yet from the first to the last every one who has taken up their study at all seriously has felt that the Trumps Major at least belonged originally neither to a game of chance nor to that other kind of chance which is called fortune-telling. They have been regarded as (1) allegorical designs containing religious and philosophical doctrine; (2) a veiled treatise on theosophy; (3) the science of the universe in hieroglyphics; (4) a keystone of occult science; (5) a summary of Kabalistic teaching; (6) the key of alchemy; and (7) the most ancient book in the world. But as these impressions have not been put forward accompanied by any tolerable evidence, it has been thought to follow in logic that Tarot cards belong to those arts in which they appear to have been used and to nothing else. In a little study of the

Tarot, accompanied by the striking designs of Miss Pamela Coleman Smith, and in its enlarged form as The Pictorial Key to the Tarot I have intimated that a secret tradition exists regarding the cards. The statement is open to every kind of misjudgment, and it is time to correct a few exaggerated inferences which have arisen out of it. An opportunity seems given by the very interesting article of Mr. J. W. Brodie-Innes, in the last issue of the OCCULT REVIEW. He has reminded me of the whole subject and has mentioned one collection of cards which are a name only to myself. I will add to my remarks certain points of fact which are not mentioned in my books.

There are in reality two Tarot traditions, or – shall I say ? – unpublished sources of knowledge: one is of the occult order, and one is purely mystical. Each of the occult sciences has a golden side of its particular shield, and this is a mystical side, alchemy being a ready case in point. The art of transmuting metals was pursued secretly, and a long line of physical adepts claim to have attained its end, their procedure being recorded in books which ex hypothesi are clear to initiates, and to no one else. But there was another school or order of research speaking the same language of symbolisms, by means of which they delineated a different quest and a distinct attainment – both of the spiritual kind. I am led to infer that this spiritual or mystical school was later, though the peculiar veil of emblems used by Zosimus the Panopolite makes one inclined to suspend judgment. After the same manner there was Operative Masonry, but there came a period – placed usually towards the end of the seventeenth century – when there arose out of it that Emblematical Art which is so familiar now among us. In this case also there are vestiges of a figurative school at an earlier period, so again it is prudent to keep an open mind. Masonry is of course occult only in an attributed sense but – as a last example – there remains Ceremonial Magic and its connections, an occult art above all and in respect both of object and procedure about the last which might be supposed to have an alternative mystical aspect; but the fact remains.

The occult tradition of the Tarot is concerned with cartomancy in so far as it belongs to the manipulation and play of the cards for fortune-telling, but it has also a curious astrological side. The mystical tradition is confined to the Trumps Major, which I have termed the Greater Arcana in my two handbooks. The occult tradition leads no one anywhere, and its mode of practice in respect of the cards is – I am told – little, if anything, better than the published kinds – so far as results are concerned. I am not of course adjudicating on this question: as a mystic I should regard all such results as worthless. A prognostication which turns out amazingly correct is of no more consequence to the soul of man than another which proves far from the mark. The occult astrology of the Tarot has naturally its divinatory side, but it is not without traces of another and deeper intention. I should think it likely that the occult tradition will "leak out," as the saying is, one of these days, for it has passed through various hands which do not seem to respect it. The mystical aspect may be explained most readily as belonging to Kabalistic theosophy, and has proved illuminating to many on the mystic quest, provided that they happen to find help in symbolism. It is precisely the same here as it is in the Churches and secret societies like Masonry. Certain are aided by its pageants of ritual, while to others they are little better than a rock of offence. The Eighteenth Degree of Rose-Croix is a hopeless adventure for those to whom ritual speaks no language, but so also is a Pontifical High Mass. Moreover, such good people would probably be well advised not to concern themselves about the mystical tradition of Tarot cards. They are not for such reason to be relegated to a lower scale and those of an opposite temperament have no warrant for assuming superiority. No one is further from God because the Ode Written in Dejection by Coleridge carries no message to his heart. There is no off or near side of the Kingdom of Heaven by these alternatives of inward character.

Such being the nature of the Tarot tradition in its two aspects there remains to be said that it has no information to offer on the time, place or circumstances of Tarot origins, nor on the question of its importation into Europe, supposing that it came from the East. There are of course expressions of opinion on the part of people who know the occult tradition, but I have not found that they are of more consequence than those of outside speculation. Speaking generally, my experience of all such traditions, when they happen to make a claim on history, is that they present mere figments of invention. The great mass of Masonic Rites and Orders have fraudulent traditional claims, and those of most Rosicrucian Societies are equally mendacious myths. Among notable exceptions are the Regime Eccosais et Rectifie – which includes the important Grades of Novice and Knight Beneficent of the Holy City – the Military and Religious Order of the

Temple, the Order of Rose-Croix of Hendover, and one mystical society which is referable in the last resort to the third quarter of the eighteenth century. As regards Craft Masonry it has worked out its own redemption by emerging from the Anderson period and its foolish fictions. If it be worth while to say so, by way of conclusion to this part of my subject, the Tarot tradition – whether mystical or occult – bears no marks of antiquity. It would not signify how old they were if they had no other claim or value, while if they offer light on any questions of the soul, it matters nothing if they are of yesterday.

On their mystical side the Trumps Major offer most notable differences from any of the known recensions, including those of Miss Coleman Smith. It will be obvious that I can offer no details; but Death, the Hanged Man, the Sun and Fool are among notable cases in point. I have said, now long ago, (1) that there are vague rumors concerning a higher meaning in the minor cards but (2) they have never yet been translated into another language than that of fortune-telling. Yet one knows not all that is doing nor always that which has been done, so it is well to add that I spoke within the measures of my own acquaintance – though I have had more than usual opportunities. In any case, the four suits of Wands, Cups, Swords and Pentacles have two strange connections in folklore, to one of which I drew attention briefly in The Hidden Church of the Holy Graal. So far as my recollection goes, I have not mentioned the other in any published work.

The four Hallows of the Holy Graal are (1) the Graal itself, understood as a Cup or Chalice, being the first Cup of the Eucharist; (2) the Spear, traditionally that of Longinus; (3) the Sword, which was made and broken under strange circumstances of allegory; and (4) the Dish of Plenty, about which the Graal tradition is composed, but it is understood generally as the Paschal Dish. The correspondence of these Hallows or Tokens with the Tarot suits will be noted, and the point is that albeit three out of the four belong to the Christian history of relics they have an antecedent folklore history belonging to the world of Celtlc myth. This is a subject which I shall hope to carry farther one of these days. There are also the four treasures of the Tuatha de Danaan: these were the Sword of the Dogda, the Spear of Lug, the Cauldron of Plenty and Lia Fail, the Stone of Destiny which indicated the rightful King. I remember one of our folk-lore scholars, and a recognized authority on the texts of Graal literature, suggesting to me that something ought be done to link these pagan talismans with the

Tarot suits, but I know as yet of no means by which the gulf of centuries can be bridged over. For the Tuatha de Danaan are of pre-Christian myth, but no one has traced Tarot cards earlier than the fourteenth century. The Tuatha de Danaan were mysterious beings of Ireland and divinities of Wales: some information concerning them will be found in Alfred Nutt's Voyage of Bran. They are said to be (1) earth-gods, (2) gods of growth and vegetation, (3) lords of the essence of life. They are connected with the idea of rebirth, usually of a god or hero.

I assume that an adequate survey of the vast field of folklore would produce other analogies, without appealing – like excellent old Court de Gebelin – to Chinese inscriptions or the avatars of Vishnu. It follows that the archaeology of the Tarot has made a beginning only and we know not whither it may lead us. Much yet remains to be done with antique packs, and I should be glad to follow up the reference of Mr. Brodie-Innes to the Clulow collection – now, as he mentions, in America. Whether it is in a public museum and whether there is a descriptive catalogue are among the first questions concerning it. One is continually coming across the titles of foreign books on Tarot and Playing Cards which might be followed up, not without profit, if we could get at the works themselves; but they are not in our public libraries. Were it otherwise, my bibliography of works dealing with the Tarot and its connections might be much extended. As regards packs, since the appearance of The Pictorial Key I have inspected a Jewish Tarot which has not, I think, been printed. It represents the black magic of divination – a most extraordinary series of designs, carrying message of evil in every sign and symbol. It is, so to speak, a Grimoire Tarot, and if it is not of French origin, the inscriptions and readings are in the French language. I have seen only the Trumps Major and two or three of the lesser Court Cards, but I understood that there is at least one complete pack in existence.

Mr. Brodie-Innes speculates as to the authority for my allocation of Tarot suits to those of ordinary playing-cards. Its source is similar to that from which Florence Emery – one of my old friends and of whom I am glad to be reminded – derived her divinatory meanings mentioned by Mr. Brodie-Innes. The source to which I refer knew well of the alternative attribution and had come to the conclusion that it was wrong. In adopting it I was careful that no allocation should be of consequence to "the outer method of the oracles" and the meanings of the Lesser Cards. Nothing follows therefore from the attribution of Swords to Clubs and Pentacles to Spades. In my book on the Graal I had already taken the other allocation of Swords to Spades and Pentacles to Clubs. I cannot say that I am especially satisfied by either mode of comparison. There is no connection in symbolism between a sword and spade, at least until the League of Nations turns all our weapons of offence into plough shares and reaping-hooks. As little correspondence appears between so-called pentacles and clubs, but it is Hobson's choice. In the absence of a canon of criticism I should prefer to say nothing as to the mystic virtues of numbers in this connection.

The Hermetic and Rosicrucian Mystery

WE are only beginning, and that by very slow stages, to enter into our inheritance from the past; and still perhaps in respect of its larger part we are seeking far and wide for the treasures of the mystic Basra. But these treasures are of more than one species and more than a single order; for that measure to which we are approximating and for that part which we hold, we shall be well advised to realize that there are some things which belong to the essences while some are of the accidents only. I do not think that among all the wise of the ages, in whatsoever regions of the world, there has been ever any difference of opinion about the true object of research; the modes and form of the quest have varied, and that widely, but to one point have all the roads converged. Therein is no change or shadow of vicissitude. We may hear of shorter roads, and one would say at first sight that such a suggestion may be true indubitably, but in one sense it is rather a convention of language and in another it is a commonplace which tends to confuse the issues. It is a convention of language because the great quests are not pursued in time or place, and it would be just as true to say that in a journey from the circumference to the centre all roads are the same length, supposing that they are straight roads. It is a commonplace because if any one should enter the byways or return on his path and restart, it is obvious that he must look to be delayed. Furthermore, it may be true that all paths lead ultimately to the centre, and that if we descend into hell there may be still a way back to the light, as if one ascended to heaven; but in any house of right reason the issues are too clear to consider such extrinsic possibilities. Before I utilize these random and, I think, too obvious considerations to present the root-thesis of this paper, I must recur for one moment to the question of the essence and the accident, because on the assumption from which the considerations originate – namely, that there is a secret tradition in Christian times, the place of which is in the West – or rather that there are several traditions – it seems desirable to realize what part matters vitally among them. I will take my illustration from alchemy, and it should be known that on the surface it claims to put forward the mystery of a material operation, behind which we discern – though not, it should be understood, invariably – another subject and another intention. Now, supposing that we were incorrect in our discernment, the secret tradition would remain, this notwithstanding, and it would remain also if the material operation were a dream not realized. But I think that a tradition of the physical kind would have no part in us, who are concerned with another conversion than that of metals, and who know that there is a mystic stone which is unseen by mortal eyes? The evidences of the secret tradition are very strong in alchemy, but it must be accepted that, either therein or other where, I am not offering the proofs that the tradition exists. There are several schools of occult literature from which it follows that something was perpetuated belonging to their own order, as, for example, the schools of magic; concerning these latter I must say what to some persons may seem a rule of excessive severity – that they embody nothing which is essential to our purpose It is time that we should set apart in our minds the domain of phenomenal occultism as something which, almost automatically, has been transferred to the proper care of science. In so doing it is our simple hope that it may continue to extend a particular class of researches into the nature of man and his environment which the unaccredited investigations of the past have demonstrated already as productive to those who can he called open to conviction. The grounds of this conviction were manifested generations or centuries ago, and along both lines the research exhibits to us from time to time that we – or some of us – who know after another manner, have been justified very surely when, as if from a more remote region, we have returned to testify that the great mysteries are within.

I have no need to affirm that the secret tradition, either in the East or the West, has been always an open secret in respect of the root-principles concerning the Way, the Truth and the Life. It is easy, therefore, to show what it is not, and to make the distinction which I have attempted between the classes of the concealed knowledge. It is not so easy to define the most precious treasures of the King – in respect of that knowledge – according to the estimate concerning them which I have assumed tacitly to be common between persons confessing to mystic predispositions at this day. The issues are confused throughout, all our high predilections notwithstanding, by the traditional or historical notion concerning the adept, which is that of a man whose power is raised to the transcendent degree by the communication or attainment, after some manner, of a particular and even terrible knowledge of the hidden forces of nature. I have heard technical and imputed adepts of occult associations state that those who possess, in the actual and plenary sense, the gifts which are ascribed to themselves by the simplicity of an artificial title, are able so to disintegrate the constituted man that they can separate not only the body from its psychic part but the spirit also from the soul, when they have a sufficient cause in their illumination against a particular victim. If things of this kind were possible, they would belong to the science of the abyss – when the abyss has been exalted above all that is termed God; but there is no need to attribute an over-great seriousness to chatter and traffic of this kind, which has been all too prevalent in a few current schools of inexactitude. The tendency contributes, as I have said, to confuse the issues and, though it may seem a perilous suggestion, one is tempted to say that, in all its higher aspects, the name itself of adept might be abandoned definitely in favor of that of the mystic – though on account of the great loose thinking it is only too likely – and there are signs sufficient already- that it would share a similar fate of misconstruction.

There was a time perhaps when we could have listened, and did even, to descriptions of this kind, because we had only just begun to hear of adepts and sages, so that things were magnified in the half-light. The scales have fallen now, and though the light into which we have entered is very far from the high light of all, it is serviceable sufficiently to dispel many shadows and to dissipate many distractions. The difficulty which is here specified is increased by the fact that there are certainly powers of the height, and that the spirit of man does not in its upward path take all the heavens of aspiration without, after some manner, being set over the kingdoms which are below it. For ourselves, at least, we can lay down one irrevocable law – that he who has resolved, setting all things else aside, to enter the path of adeptship must look for his progress in proportion as he pursues holiness for its own sake and not for the miracles of sanctity. It will be seen that I am disposed to call things by their old names, which have many consecrations, and I hope to command sympathy – but something more even – when I say further that he who dreams of adeptship and does not say sanctity in his heart till his lips are cleansed and then does not say it with his lips, is not so much far from the goal as without having conceived regarding it. One of the lesser masters, who has now scarcely a pupil amongst us, said once, quoting from somewhere *Yel sanctum invenit, vel sanctvm facit*; but I know that it must be long resident in our desires before it can he declared in our lives.

I have searched the whole West and only in two directions have I found anything which will compare with pure monastic mysticism; one of these is the mystic side of alchemy, while the other is that body of tradition which answers most fully to the name of Rosicrucianism. There are other places in which we find the same thing, or the substance of the same thing, and I believe that I have given faithful testimony already on this point; even in the lesser schools I am sure that it was always at the roots, but except in so far as a personal sympathy may direct us, or the accidents of an historical study, I do not know that there is a direct gain- or that there is not rather a hindrance – by going any distance afield for what is so close to our hands, and into side issues for what is in the straight road – whether this be broad or narrow. There is no doubt that from one point of view Christian mysticism has been on the external side bewared rather seriously by its environment, because of the inhibitions of the official churches in saying this, I hope that the time has come to all of us when the cheap conventions of hostility towards these churches, and especially towards the Latin Rite, have ceased to obtain in our minds and that we can appreciate, in however detached a manner, the high annals of their sanctity. If so, we shall be able to appreciate also, at the proper value, an external and historical side on which the Latin Church approached too often that picture in the story of the Holy Graal of a certain King of Castle Mortal, who sold God for money. The difficulty which the Rite has created and the inhibitions into which it has passed arise more especially not alone on the external side but from the fact that it has taken the great things of symbolism too generally for material facts. In this way, with all the sincerity which can be attached to its formal documents, produced for the most part by the process of growth, the Church Catholic of Latin Christianity has told the wrong story, though the elements which were placed in its hands are the right and true elements. I believe that the growth of sanctity within the Latin Church has been- under its deepest consideration substantially hindered by the over-encrustation of the spirit with the literal aspect, though this at the same time is indispensable to expression. I believe that in the minds of the mystics this hindrance has operated; of all men on earth they have recognized assuredly the working of the spirit; but they sought to attain it through the veils of doctrine and they did not utterly and wholly part the curtains thereof. The result was that these trailed after them and were an impediment as they entered the sanctuary. The process itself was, in one sense, the wrong process, though on account of their environment it was almost impossible that they should adopt another. We have agreed long ago that to work up from Nature to Grace is not really the method of the wise, because that which is below is the branches and that which is above is the roots, and the tree of life is really in this sense, and because of our distance from the centre, as it were, upside down. So also the true way of experience in the mystic life is to work outward from within. It is natural, of course, and this is of necessity also, that we should receive our first intimations through the letter, but when it has exhibited to us some reflections of the light which is behind we must not suffer our course to be hindered by the office of the letter, but should set it aside rather, to abide in the root-meaning which is behind the symbols. There is a later stage in which we shall revert to the external and to the meaning that is without, bringing back with us the inward light to interpenetrate and transform it. Perhaps an illustration will explain better the order of procedure than a formal statement merely, though I do not think that there is even a surface difficulty concerning it. We have been taught in the infancy of the mind the great story which is the root and heart of external Christianity. That is not the letter which kills but the cortex of a vessel behind which are the eternal fountains of life. I need not say that many of us do not get beyond this cortex and, fortunately, it is not a dead husk, but a living body through which Grace flows to us after the measure of our capacity. But it may come to pass that the inward sensorium is opened – by the mediation, as it may well be, of the great books of the Church, or in what manner soever – and we then see that the great story, the old story, the story which is of all things true, is that of our own soul. I mean this not in the sense of the soul's geniture, but in the sense of its progress, as it is here and now environed. We are then looking towards the real road of our redemption, and it is at this stage that the letter should be set aside for a period because everything has to be enacted anew. The virgin must conceive and bear her son; in the grand rough outline of Saint Martin the son must be born in the Bethlehem of our human life; he must be presented in the temple which stands in the Jerusalem within; he must confound the doctors of the intellect; he must lead the hidden life of Nazareth; he must be manifested and must teach us within, in which way we shall return to the world of doctrine and shall find that all things are made new. It is not that there are new doctrines, but there is another quality of life; thereby the old symbolism has been so interpenetrated that the things which are without have become the things which are within, till each seems either in the power of the grace and in the torrent of the life. It is then that we cease to go out through the door by which we went in, because other doors are open, and the call of many voices, bidding us no longer depart hence, says rather: Let us enter the sanctuary, even the inmost shrine.

I desire, therefore, to make it plain that the Secret Church Mystic which exists and has always existed within the Church Militant of Christendom does not differ in anything from the essential teaching of doctrine – I mean *Quod semper, quod ubique, quod ab omnibus*; that it can say with its heart what it says also with its lips; that again there is no change or shadow of vicissitude; but in some very high sense the ground of the essentials has been removed. The symbolism remains; it has not taken on another meaning; hut it has unfolded itself like the flower from within. Christian Theosophy in the West can recite its

Credo in unum Deum by clause and by clause, including in *unam sanctum catholicam et apostolicam ecclesiam*, and if there is an *arriere pensee* it is not of heresy or Jesuitry. Above all, and I say this the more expressly because there are still among us – that is to say, in those circles generally – certain grave misconceptions, and it is necessary to affirm that the path of the mystic does not pass through the heresies.

And now with respect to the secret schools which have handed down to us at this day some part or aspects of the secret tradition belonging to Christian times, I must leave out of consideration, because there are limits to papers of this kind, the great witness of Kabalism which although it is a product of the Christian period is scarcely of it, and although therein the quest and its term do not assuredly differ from that of the truth which is in Christ, there are perhaps other reasons than those of brevity for setting it apart here. Alchemy may not have originated much further East than Alexandria, or, alternatively, it may have travelled from China when the port of Byzantium was opened to the commerce of the world. In either case, its first development, in the forms with which we are acquainted, is connected with the name of Byzantium, and the earliest alchemists of whom we have any remains in literature constitute a class by themselves under the name of Byzantine alchemists. The records of their processes went into Syria and Arabia, where they assumed a new mode, which bore, however, all necessary evidence of its origin. In this form it does not appear to have had a specific influence upon the *corpus doctrinale*. The records were also taken West, like many other mysteries of varying importance, and when they began to assume a place in western history this was chiefly in France, Germany and England. In other words, there arose the cycle of Latin alchemy, passing at a later date, by the way of translation, into the vernaculars of the respective countries, until finally, but much later, we have original documents in English, French and German. It follows, but has not so far been noticed, that the entire literature is a product of Christian times and has Christianity as its motive, whether subconsciously or otherwise. This statement applies to the Latin Geber and the tracts which are ascribed to Morien and Rhasis. The exception which proves the rule is the Kabalistic Aesh Mezareph, which we know only by fragments included in the great collection of Rosenroth. I suppose that there is no labyrinth which it is quite so difficult to thread as that of the *Theatrum Chemicum.* It is beset on every side with pitfalls, and its clues, though not destroyed actually, have been buried beneath the ground. Expositors of the subject have gone astray over the general purpose of the art, because some have believed it to be: (a) the transmutation of metals, and that only, while others have interpreted it as (b) a veiled method of delineating the secrets of the soul on its way through the world within, and besides this nothing. Many textbooks of physical alchemy would seem to have been re-edited in this exotic interest. The true philosophers of each school are believed to have taught the same thing, with due allowance for the generic difference of their term, and seeing that they use the same language it would seem that, given a criterion of distinction in respect of the term, this should make the body of cryptogram comparatively easy to disentangle. But as one of the chief difficulties is said also to reside in the fact that many of them do not begin at the same point of the process, the advantage of uniformity is cancelled largely.

There are affirmed to be experimental schools still existing in Europe which have carried the physical work much further than it is ever likely to be taken by any isolated student; but this must be accepted under several reserves, or I can say, at least, that, having better occasions than most people of knowing the schools and their development, I have so far found no evidence. But there are testified otherwise to be – and I speak here with the certainty of first-hand knowledge – other schools, also experimental, also existing in Europe, which claim to possess the master-key of the mystical work. How far they have been successful at present in using that key I am not in a position to say, nor can I indicate its nature for reasons that, I think, must be obvious. It so happens, however, that the mystery of the processes is one thing and that which lies on the surface, or more immediately beneath the externals of the concealed language, is, fortunately, another thing. And, as often happens also, the enlightening correspondences are offering their marks and seals – if not at our very doors – at least in the official churches. Among all those places that are holy there is no holy place in which they do not abide a *mane usque ad vespertinum*, and the name of the correspondence-in-chief is the Holy Eucharist.

I propose now to tabulate certain palmary points of terminology which are common to all the adepts, including both schools indifferently, though we are dealing here – and this is understood – with the process of one school only. By the significance of these points or terms we shall see to what extent the symbolism of the higher alchemy is in conformity with mystic symbolism and with the repose of the life of the Church in God. It should be realized, however, that there is nothing so hard and so thankless as to elucidate one symbolism by the terms of another- and this notwithstanding an occasional identity which may manifest in the terms of each.

It must be understood further and accepted that all alchemists, outside the distinctions of their schools, were actuated by an express determination to veil their mystery and that they had recourse for this purpose to every kind of subterfuge. At the same time they tell us that the whole art is contained, manifested and set forth by means of a single vessel, which, amidst all manner of minor variations, is described with essential uniformity throughout the great multitude of texts. This statement constitutes a certain lesser key to the art; but as on the one hand the alchemists veil their hallow-in-chief by reference, in spite of their assurance, as above noted, to many pretended vessels, so has the key itself a certain aspect of subterfuge, since the alleged unity is in respect only of the term final of the process in the unity of the recipient. This unity is the last reduction of a triad, because, according to these aspects of Hermetic philosophy, man in the course of his attainment is at first three – that is, when he sets out upon the great quest; he is two at a certain stage; but he is, in fine, one, which is the end of his evolution. The black state of the matter on which the process of the art is engaged is the body of this death, from which the adepts have asked to be detached. It is more especially our natural life. The white state of the stone, the confection of which is desired, is the vesture of immortality with which the epopts are clothed upon. The salt of the philosophers is that savor of life without which the material earth can neither be salted nor cleansed. The sulphur of the philosophers is the inward substance by which some souls are saved, yet so as by fire. The mercury of the sages is that which must be fixed and volatilized- naturally it is fluidic and wandering- but except under this name, or by some analogous substitute, it must not be described literally outside the particular circles of secret knowledge. It is nearer than hands and feet.

Now the perfect correspondence of these things in the symbolism of official Christianity, and the great mystery of perfect sanctification, is set forth in the great churches under the sacramentalism of the Holy Eucharist. This is my point, and I desire to make it clear: the same exalted mystery which lies behind the symbols of bread and wine, behind the undeclared priesthood which is according to the order of Melchisedeck, was expressed by the alchemists under the guise of transmutation; but I refer here to the secret school of adeptship which had taken over in another and transcendent interest the terminology and processes of occult metallurgy.

The vessel is therefore one, but the matter thereto adapted is not designated especially, or at least after an uniform manner it is said to be clay by those who speak at times more openly in order that they may be understood the less, as if they also were singing in their strange chorus: –

Let us be open as the day,
That we may deeper hide ourselves.

It is most commonly described as metallic, because on the surface of the literature there is the declared mystery of all metals, and the concealed purpose is to show that in the roots and essence of these things there is a certain similarity or analogy. The reason is that the epopt, who has been translated, again finds his body after many days, but under a great transmutation, as if in another sense the *panis quotidianis* had been changed into the panis *virus et vita* / is, but without mutation of the accidents. The reason is also that in normal states the body is here and now not without the soul, nor can we separate readily, by any intellectual process, the soul from the spirit which broods there over, to fertilize it in a due season. It is, however, one vessel, and this makes for simplicity; hut it is not by such simplicity that the art is testified to be a *lusus puerorum*. The contradistinction hereto is that it is hard to be a Christian, which is the comment of the man born blind upon the light that he cannot see. There is also the triumphant affirmation of the mystical counter-position, that to sin is hard indeed for the man who knows truly. The formula of this is that man is born for the heights rather than the deeps, and its verbal paradox is *facilis ascensus superno*. The process of the art is without haste or violence by the mediation of a graduated fire, and the seat of this fire is in the soul. It is a mystery of the soul's love, and for this reason she is called "undaunted daughter of desire." The sense of the gradation is that love is set free from the impetuosity and violence of passion and has become a constant and incorruptible flame. The formula of this is that the place of unity is a centre wherein there is no exaggeration. That which the fire consumes is certain materials or elements, which are called *recrementa*, the grosser parts, the superfluities; and it should he observed that there are two purgations, of which the first is the gross and the second the subtle. The first is the common process of conversion, by which there is such a separation of seemingly external components that what remains is as a new creature, and may be said to be reborn. The second is the exalted conversion, by which that which has been purified is so raised that it enters into a new region, or a certain heaven comes down and abides therein. It is not my design in the present place to exhaust all the sources of interpretation, because such a scheme would be impossible in a single paper, and I can allude, therefore, but scantily to the many forms of the parables which are concerned with the process up to this point. The ostensible object, which was materialized in the alternative school, is the confection of a certain stone or powder, which is that of projection, and the symbolical theorem is that this powder, when added to a base metal, performs the wonder of transmutation into pure silver or gold, better than those of the mines. Otherwise, it prolongs life and renews youth in the adept- philosopher and lover of learning. In the second case, it is spoken of usually as an elixir, but the transmuting powder and the renewing draught are really one thing with the spiritual alchemists. It must be also affirmed that in virtue of a very high mysticism there is an unity in the trinity of the powder, the metal and the vase. The vase is also the alchemist on his outer side, for none of the instruments, the materials, the fires, the producer, and the thing produced are external to the one subject. At the same time the inward man is distinguished from the outward man; we may say that the one is the alchemist and the other the vessel. It is in this sense that the art is both physical and spiritual. But the symbolism is many times enfolded, and the gross metal which is placed within the vessel is the untransmuted life of reason, motive, concupiscence, self-interest and all that which constitutes the intelligent creature on the normal plane of manifestation. Hereof is the natural man enclosed in an animal body, as the metal is placed in the vessel, and from this point of view the alchemist is he who is sometimes termed arrogantly the superman. But because there is only one vessel it must be understood that herein the stone is confected and the base metal is converted. The alchemist is himself finally the stone, and because many zealous aspirants to the art have not understood this they have failed in the great work on the spiritual side. The schedule which now follows may elucidate this hard subject somewhat more fully and plainly.

There are (a) the natural, external man, whose equivalent is the one vessel; (b) the body of desire, which answers to the gross matter; (c) the aspiration, the consciousness, the will of the supernatural life; (d) the process of the will working on the body of desire within the outward vessel; (e) the psychic and transcendental conversion thus effected; (f) the reaction of the purified body of desire on the essential will, so that the one supports the other, while the latter is borne upward, and from such raising there follows this further change, that the spirit of a man puts on itself a new quality of life, becoming an instrument which is at once feeding and is itself fed; (g) herein is the symbol of the stone and the great elixir; (h) the spirit is nourished from above by the analogies of Eucharistic ministry; (i) the spirit nourishes the soul, as by bread and wine; (j) the soul effects the higher conversion in the body of desire; (k) it thus comes about that the essence which dissolves everything and changes everything is still contained in a vessel, or – alternatively – that God abides in man.

This process, thus exhaustively delineated in the parables of alchemy, is put with almost naked simplicity by Eucharistic doctrine, which says that material lips receive the supersubstantial bread and wine, that the soul is nourished and that Christ enters the soul. It seems, therefore, within all reason and all truth to testify that the *panis vivus et vitalis* is even as the transmuting stone and that the chalice of the new and eternal testament is as the renewing elixir; but I say this under certain reasonable reserves because, in accordance with my formal indication, the closer the analogies between distinct systems of symbolism the more urgent is that prudence which counsels us not to confuse them by an interchangeable use.

All Christian mysticism came forth out of the Mass Book, and it returns therein. But the Mass Book in the first instance came out of the heart mystic which had unfolded in Christendom. The nucleus of truth in the missal is *Dominus prope est*. The Mass shows that the great work is in the first sense a work of the hands of man, because it is he officiating as a priest in his own temple who offers the sacrifice which he has purified. But the elements of that sacrifice are taken over by an intervention from another order, and that which follows is transfusion.

Re-expressing all this now in a closer summary, the apparatus of mystical alchemy is indeed, comparatively speaking, simple.

The first matter is myrionimous and is yet one, corresponding to the unity of the natural will and the unlimited complexity of its motives, dispositions, desires, passions and distractions, on all of which the work of wisdom must operate. The vessd is also one, for this is the normal man complete in his own degree. The process has the seal of Nature's directness; it is the graduation and increasing maintenance of a particular fire. The initial work is a change in the substance of will, aspiration and desire, which is the first conversion or transmutation in the elementary sense.

But it is identical even to the end with the term proposed by the Eucharist, which is the modification of the nominal man by the communication of Divine Substance. Here is the *lapis qui non lapis, lapis tingens, lapis angularis, lapis qui multiplicetur, lapis per quem justus aedificabit domum Domini, et jam valde aedificatur et terram possidebit, per omnia*, etc. When it is said that the stone is multiplied, even to a thousand-fold, we know that this is true of all seed which is sown upon good soil.

So, therefore, the stone transmutes and the Eucharist transmutes also; the philosophical elements on the physical side go to the making of the stone which is also physical; and the sacramental elements to the generation of a new life in the soul. He who says Lapis Philosophorum, says also: My beloved to me and I to him: Christ is therefore the stone, and the stone in adept humanity is the union realized, while the great secret is that Christ must be manifested within.

Now it seems to me that it has not served less than an useful purpose to establish after a new manner the intimate resemblance between the higher understanding of one part of the secret tradition and the better interpretation of one sacrament of the church. It must be observed that we are not dealing in either case with the question of attainment. The analogy would remain if spiritual alchemy and Christian sacramentalism abode in the intellectual order as theorems only, or as part of the psychic dream which had never been carried into experience. It would be more easy (if there were here any opportunity) to offer the results of the experience as recorded in the lives of the saints than to discuss the traditional attainments which are held to have passed into actuality among the secret schools; but the veiled literatures must be left to speak for themselves, which – for those who can read – they do, like the annals of sanctity as to these – those who will take the pains may seek verification for themselves. My task in respect of spiritual alchemy ends by exhibiting that this also was a mystery of sanctity concerned ex hypothesis with the communication of Divine Substance, and that this is the term of the Eucharist. It is this which the doctrine of sanctity offered, to those who entered the pathway of sanctity, as the foretaste in this life of the union which is consummated in eternity, or of that end beyond which there is nothing whatever which is conceivable. We know from the old books that it has not entered into the heart of man, but the heart which has put away the things of sense conceives it by representations and types. This is the great tradition of that which the early alchemists term truth in the art; the end is representation after its own kind rather than felicity, but the representation is of that order which begins in ecstasy and ends in absorption. Let no man say, therefore, that he loses himself in experience of this order, for, perchance, it is then only that he finds himself, even in that way which suggests that after many paths of activity he is at length coming into his own.

It might seem that I have reached here a desirable point for my conclusion, but I am pledged, alike by my title and one antecedent reference, to say something concerning Rosicrucianism, which is another witness in the world on the part of the secret tradition. There is one respect in which it is simpler in its apparatus than the literature of the purely Hermetic tradition, for it lies within a smaller compass and has assumed a different mode. It is complicated by the fact that very few of the texts which are available among the things of the outside world have a title to rank in its tradition. This, I suppose, is equivalent to an intimation that the witness is still in the world after another and more active manner, which is true in more than a single way. I am not the ambassador, and much less the plenipotentiary, of the secret societies in the West, and independently of this statement I feel sure that I shall not be accused of endeavoring to assume the role or to create the impression. I know only that the societies exist, and that they are at the present time one means of perpetuating that tradition. I do not suggest that there are no other means, because I have indicated even from the beginning that the door looking towards heaven and the sanctuary which is its ante-chamber was opened long centuries ago by the official churches. But the tradition itself has been rather behind the churches and some part of the things for which we are all seeking is to he found therein- all which is without detriment to the light of the East, because this is also the light of the West under another veil. Even in the esoteric assemblies which are now and here among us, the tradition is, in a sense, veiled, and, of course, in speaking publicly one has always to cloud the sanctuaries rather than to say: Lift up your eyes, for it is in this or that corner of London, Paris or Prague.

If there is one thing more regrettable than the confusion in forms of symbolism, it is the identification of separate entities under a general term which has only a particular meaning so far as history is concerned. The name Rosicrucian, has suffered from abuse of this kind, being used almost interchangeably with that of Alchemist by popular writers. I must ask to be disassociated from this error when I say that the external history of the Rosy Cross, in so far as it can be said to exist, has only one point of correspondence with Rosicrucian traditions perpetuated by secret societies in a few centers of Europe. The point of correspondence is the legend-in-chief of the Order, detached from the pseudo-historical aspect which it bore in the early documents, and associated with a highly advanced form of symbolism. It is in this form only that it enters into the sequence of the mysteries, and exhibits how the priest-king does issue from Salem, carrying bread and wine. We have, therefore, the Eucharistic side in the higher Rosicrucian tradition, but if I may describe that which is greater in the terms of that which is lesser- because of the essential difficulty with which I am confronted- it has undergone a great change, not by a diminution of the sacraments but because they are found everywhere. The alchemical maxim which might be inscribed over the gate of any Rosicrucian temple is – *Est in Mercurio quicquid quaerunt sapientes.*

The Eucharistic maxim which might be written over the laboratory of the alchemist, in addition to *Laborare ese orare*, would be-

Et antiquum documentum Novo cedat ritui:
Praestet fides supplementum Sensuum defectui.

The maxim which might be written over the temples of the official churches is *Corporis Mysterium*, that the mystery of the body might lead them more fully into the higher mystery of the soul. And, in fine, that maxim which might, and will be, inscribed over the one temple of the truly catholic religion when the faiths of this western world have come into their own- that which is simplest of all, and of all most pregnant, would be *mysterium fidei*, the mystery which endures for ever and for ever passes into experience.

In conclusion as to this part, Rosicrucianism is the mystery of that which dies in manifestation that the life of the manifest may be ensured. I have found nothing in symbolism which accounts like Rose-Cross symbolism for that formula which on one side is the summary expression of mysticism: "And I look for the resurrection of the dead and the life of the world to come."

And now in conclusion generally: –

I have spoken of three things only, and of one of them with great brevity, because the published literatures have to be set aside, and of that which remains it does not appear in the open face of day. The initiations are many and so are the schools of thought, but those which are true schools and those which are high orders issue from one root. *Est una sola res*, and those whose heart of contemplation is fixed upon this one thing may differ widely but can never be far apart. Personally, I do not believe- and this has the ring of a commonplace- that if they came to understand one another they would be found to differ widely. I know not what systems of the eons may intervene between that which is imperishable within us and the union wherein the universe will, in fine, repose at the centre. But I know that the great systems ay, even the great processes – of the times that are gone, as of those which now encompass us – do not pass away, because that which was from the beginning, is now and ever shall be- is one motive, one aspiration, one term of thought remaining, as if in the stillness of an everlasting present. We really understand one another, and our collective aspirations are united, world without end.

The Pictorial Symbols of Alchemy

THE Hermetic Mystery – upon the higher interpretation of which I have spoken at considerable length in the previous paper and have created an analogy between its hidden meaning and that which I should term the centre of the Religions Mystery in Christendom – is the only branch of mystic and occult literature which lent itself to the decorative sense. I suppose that there are few people comparatively who at this day have any notion of the extent to which that sense was developed in the books of the adepts. It will be understood that in speaking now upon this subject I am leaving my proper path, but though the fact does not seem to have been registered, it is so utterly curious to note how a literature which is most dark and inscrutable of all has at the same time its lighter side- a side, indeed, of pleasant inventions, of apologue, of parable, of explicit enigma, above all of poetry. The fact is that alchemy presented itself as an art, its books were the work of artists; and for the sympathetic reader, even when he may understand them least, they will read sometimes like enchanting fables or legends. When in this manner some of the writers had exhausted their resources in language, they had recourse to illustrations, and I wonder almost that no one has thought to collect the amazing copper-plates which literally did adorn the Latin and other tracts of the seventeenth century.

As I propose to print some selected specimens of the pictorial art in alchemy because they are exceedingly curious, and not for a deeper reason, the reader will not expect, and for once in a way will perhaps be rather relieved, that I am not going in quest especially of their inner meanings. So far as may be possible, the pictures shall speak for themselves, seeing that I write for the moment rather as a lover of books – a bibliophile – than a lover of learning. I will begin, however, with a definition. The alchemists whom I have in my mind may be classified as artists on the decorative side and in their illustrations – but I know not whether they were their own draughtsmen – they approached the Rabelaisian method. The school on both sides is rather of Germanic origin; and it is such entirely, so far as the pictures are concerned. The French alchemists had recourse occasionally to designs, but they are negligible for the present purpose. This is a clearance of the ground, but it must be added that the great and authoritative textbooks have not been illustrated- as, for example, The Open Entrance to the Closed Palace of the King, which is the work of Eirenaeus Philalethes, and the *New Light of Alchemy*, which is believed to be that of. Alexander Seton. If I may attempt such a comparison, Philalethes – in the work mentioned- reads rather like a Pauline epistle and Seton like an Epistle to the Hebrews but the analogy in both cases is intended to be allusive only, and strict in no sense. So also they read here and there as if they were almost inspired; but they could not be termed decorative. The really practical works – as, for example, the Latin treatises ascribed to Geber – are never illustrated, except by crude sketches of material vessels used in the material art for the aid of the neophyte on his way to the transmutation of metals. I do not think that they really helped him, and they are of no account for our purpose. The pictures of the adepts were the allegorical properties of the adepts, and though the criticism has a side of harshness they were almost obviously provided for the further confusion of the inquirer, under the pretence of his enlightenment. At the same time, authors or artists were sages after their own manner, their allegories had a set purpose and represent throughout a prevailing school of symbolism.

It is quite easy to work out the elementary part of the symbolism; it is not difficult to speculate reasonably about some of the more obscure materials. But the true canons of alchemical criticism yet remain to be expounded; and I believe that I have intimated otherwise the difficulty and urgency attaching to this work, so that there may be one unerring criterion to distinguish between the texts representing the spiritual and those of the physical work. On the latter phase of the subject it would be useless – and more than useless – to discourse in any periodical, even if I could claim to care anything and to know sufficiently thereof. I know neither enough to hold my tongue nor enough to speak, so that I differ in this respect – but for once only – from my excellent precursor Elias Ashmole. Like him and like Thomas Vaughan, I do know the narrowness of the name Chemia, with the antiquity and infinity of the proper object of research; thereon we have all borne true witness in our several days and generations.

It is a matter of common report that the old Hermetic adepts were the chemists of their time and that, as such, they made numerous and valuable discoveries. This is true in a general sense, but under what is also a general and an exceedingly grave reserve. There is little need to say in the first place, that the spiritual alchemists made no researches and could have had no findings in the world of metals and minerals. Secondly, there was a great concourse of witnesses in secret literature, who were adepts of neither branch; but they expressed their dreams and speculations in terms of spurious certitude, and were often sincere in the sense that they deceived themselves. They produced sophistications in the physical work and believed that their tinctures and colorations were the work of philosophy; these discovered nothing, and misled nearly every one. They also – in the alternative school – pursued erroneous ways or translated their aspirations at a distance into root-matter of spiritual Hermetic tradition; they reached the term of their folly and drew others who were foolish after them, who had also no law of differentiation between things of Caesar and God. Finally – but of these I say nothing – there were arrant impostors, representing the colportage of their time, who trafficked in the interest of the curious, assuming alchemy for their province, as others of the secret sciences were exploited by others of their kindred. Now, between all these the official historians of chemistry in the near past had no ground of distinction, and there is little certainty that they were right over many or most of their judgments.

Once more, the canon was wanting; as I have shown that in another region it is either wanting for ourselves, or – to be correct – is in course only of development. This work, therefore, was largely one of divination, with a peculiar uncertainty in the results.

I have now finished with this introductory part, and I offer in the first place a simple illustration of the alchemist's laboratory, as it was conceived by Michael Maier at the beginning of the seventeenth century. He had a hand in the Rosicrucianism of his period and published some laws of the brotherhood, or alternatively those of an incorporated sodality based on similar lines. He was a man of great and exceptional learning, but withal of a fantastic spirit; he is proportionately difficult to judge, but his palmary concern was the material side of the magnum opus. He may have veered, and did probably, into other directions. The illustration is chosen from The Golden Tripod, being three ancient tracts attributed respectively to Basil Valentine, Thomas Norton, and John Cremer – a so – called abbot of Westminster. It is these personages who are apparently represented in the picture, together with the zelator, servant or pupil, attached to the master of the place, whose traditional duty was the maintenance with untiring zeal of the graduated fire of the art. Basil Valentine, in the course of his tract, makes it clear that he is concerned therein only with the physical work, and in the decorative manner which I have mentioned he affirms that if the three alchemical principles – namely, philosophical Mercury, Sulphur and Salt – can be rectified till "the metallic spirit and body are joined together inseparably by means of the metallic soul," the chain of love will he riveted firmly thereby and the palace prepared for the coronation.

But the substances in question are not those which are known under these names, and it is for this reason, or for reasons similar thereto, that no process of metallic alchemy can be followed practically by the isolated student, because everything essential is left out. The tradition is that the true key was imparted only from the adept to his son in the art. This notwithstanding, Basil Valentine calls the particular work to which I am here referring, The Twelve Keys, and it is said that they open the twelve doors leading to the Stone of the Philosophers and to the true Medicine. The same terminology would be used by the spiritual alchemists in another and higher sense; but this school possesses a master-key which opens all the doors. Basil Valentine's second key is that of Mercury, as it is pictured here below.

This, it will be seen, is the crowned or philosophical Mercury, bearing in either hand the caduceus, which is his characteristic emblem, and having wings upon his shoulders, signifying the volatilized state. But there are also wings beneath his feet, meaning that he has overcome this state, and has been fixed by the art of the sages, which is part of the Great Work, requiring the concurrence of the Sun and Moon, whose symbols appear behind him. The figures at either side carry on their wands or swords respectively the Bird of Hermes and a crowned serpent. The latter corresponds to that serpent which, by the command of Moses, was uplifted in the wilderness for the healing of the children of Israel. As in this figure Mercury has become a constant fire, one of the figures is shielding his face from the brilliance. He is on the side of the increasing moon, but on the side of the sun is he who has attained the Medicine, and he looks therefore with a steadfast face upon the unveiled countenance of the vision. According to Basil Valentine, Mercury is the principle of life. He says also that Saturn is the chief key of the art, though it is least useful in the mastery. The reference is to philosophical lead, and he gives a very curious picture representing this key, as it is shown on the next page [here below. Ed.].

The King in Basil Valentine's terminology is the stone in its glorious rubefaction, or state of redness, when it is surrounded by the whole court of the metals. The Spouse of the King is Venus; Saturn is the Prefect of the royal household; Jupiter is the Grand Marshal; Mars is at the head of military affairs; Mercury has the office of Chancellor; the Sun is Vice-Regent; the office of the Moon is not named, but she seems to be a Queen in widowhood. Before them there is borne the banner attributed to each: that of the King is crimson, emblazoned with the figure of Charity in green garments; that of Saturn- which is carried by Astronomy – is black, emblazoned with the figure of Faith in garments of yellow and red; that of Jupiter – which is carried by Rhetoric- is grey, emblazoned with Hope in party-colored garments; that of Mars is crimson, with Courage in a crimson cloak, and it is borne by Geometry; that of Mercury is carried by Arithmetic, and is a rainbow standard with the figure of Temperance, also in a many-colored vestment; that of the Sun is a yellow banner, held by Grammar and exhibiting the figure of Justice in a golden robe; that of the Moon is resplendent silver, with the figure of Prudence, clothed in sky-blue, and it is borne by. Dialectic. Venus has no banner apart from that of the King, but her apparel is of gorgeous magnificence.

I pass now to another order of symbolism which delineates the spiritual work by means of very curious pictures, accompanied by evasive letterpress. These are also from a Germanic source, and the writer-if not the designer-was Nicholas Barnaud, who went among many others in quest of Rosicrucians, but it does not appear what he found. I will give in the first place a Symbol which represents Putrefaction, being the disintegration of the rough matter in physical alchemy and on the spiritual side the mystery of mystical death.

According to The Book of Lambspring, which is the name of the little treatise, the sages keep close guard over the secret of this operation, because the world is unworthy; and the children of philosophy, who receive its communication in part and carry it to the proper term by their personal efforts, enjoy it also in silence, since God wills that it should be hidden. This is the conquest of the dragon of material and manifest life; but it is like the old folklore fables, in which an act of violence is necessary to determine an enchantment for the redemption of those who are enchanted. The work is to destroy the body, that the body may not only be revived, but may live henceforth in a more perfect and as if incorruptible form. The thesis is that Nature is returned unto herself with a higher gift and more sacred warrant and the analogy among things familiar is the sanctification of intercourse by the sacrament of marriage. The dragon in this picture is destroyed by a knight, but we shall understand that he is clothed in the armor of God, and that St. Paul has described the harness.

The next illustration concerns the natural union between body soul and spirit; it is represented pictorially in the tract after more than one manner, as when two fishes are shown swimming in the sea, and it is said that the sea is the body. Here it is a stag and an unicorn, while the body is that forest which they range. The unicorn represents the spirit, and he who can couple them together and lead them out of the forest deserves to be called a Master, as the letterpress testifies.

The reason is that on their return to the body the flesh itself will he changed and will have been rendered golden. In respect of the alternative illustration, the mystery of this reunion is likened to a work of coaction, by which the three are so joined together that they are not afterwards sundered; and this signifies the Medicine. In yet another picture the spirit and soul are represented by a lion and lioness, between which a union must be effected before the work upon the body can be accomplished.

It is an operation of great wisdom and even cunning, and he who performs it has merited the need of praise before all others. I suppose that rough allegory could hardly express more plainly the marriage in the sanctified life between the human soul and the Divine Part. Neither text nor illustration continue so clear in the sequel, more especially as different symbols are used to represent the same things. In the next picture the war between the soul and the spirit is shown by that waged between a wolf and a dog, till one of them kills the other, and a poison is thus generated which restores them in some obscure manner, and they become the great and precious Medicine which in its turn restores the sages.

The tract then proceeds to the consideration of Mercury, and to all appearance has changed its subject, though this is not really the case, as might be demonstrated by an elaborate interpretation; but I omit this and the pictures thereto belonging, not only from considerations of space but because the task would be difficult, since it is not possible to say what the spiritual alchemists intended by Mercury, this being the secret of a particular school. When the sequence is again taken up the human trinity is presented under another veil, being that of the Father, the Son and the Guide. The symbolism is strangely confused, but some apologists would affirm that this was for a special purpose. In any case, the soul now appears as a boy; the Guide is the Spirit, and the illustration shows them at the moment of parting, when the soul is called to ascend, so that it may understand all wisdom and go even to the gate of Heaven. Their hands are interlinked, and it will he seen that the highest of all is distinguished- except for his wings- by an utter simplicity, characterized by his plain vestments. He, on the other hand, who represents the body has the symbols of earthly royalty.

The story concerning them tells how the Soul ascended till it beheld the throne of Heaven. The next picture is intended to set forth this vision, when the soul and spirit are seen on the high mountain of initiation, with all the splendors of the celestial canopy exhibited above them.

It is said to be a mountain in India, which in books of the Western adepts seems always to have been regarded as the symbolical soul's home and the land of epopts. The text states, notwithstanding, that the mountain lies in the vessel, and those who remember what was set forth in my previous paper will know exactly what this means – an intimation on the part of the alchemist that lie is dealing only with events of experience belonging to the world within. That which is expressed, however, as a result of the vision is that the soul remembers the body-spoken of here as the father- and longs to return thereto, to which the Spirit Guide consents, and they descend from that high eminence. Two things are illustrated hereby – (1) that the soul in its progress during incarnate life has the body to save and to change, so that all things may be holy; but (2) that it is possible – as is nearly always the case in parables of this kind – to offer a dual interpretation, and the alternative to that which I have given would be an allegory of return to the House of the Father in an entirely different sense. But it is obvious that I cannot speak of it – at least, in the present place. The next picture – and assuredly the most grotesque of all – represents the reunion of body and soul by the extraordinary process of the one devouring the other, during which operation it should he noted that the spirit stands far apart.

The text now approaches its close and delineates the construction of a reborn and glorified body, as the result of which it is said "The son ever remains in the father, and the father in the son... By the grace of God they abide for ever, the father and the son triumphing gloriously in the splendor of their new Kingdom." They sit upon one throne and between them is the spirit, the Ancient Master, who is arrayed in a crimson robe. So is the triadic union accomplished, and herein is the spiritual understanding of that mystery which is called the Medicine in terms of alchemical philosophy.

The finality of the whole subject can be expressed in a few words, and although it may be a dark saying for some of my readers it may prove a light to others, and for this reason I give it as follows: The experiment of spiritual alchemy was the Yoga process of the West. The root-reason of the statement must be already, as I think, obvious -probably from the present paper and assuredly from that which preceded it. The physical experiment of the magnum opus may have been carried in the past to a successful issue. I do not know, and of my concern it is no part; but those who took over the terminology of the transmutation of metals and carried it to another degree had opened gates within them which lead into the attainment of all desire in the order which is called absolute, because after its attainment all that we understand by the soul's dream has passed into the soul's reality. It is the dream of Divine Union, and eternity cannot exhaust the stages of its fulfillment

Restoration

I CAME into the world for love of Thee,
I left Thee at Thy bidding;
I put off my white robes and shining crown
And came into this world for love of Thee.

I have lived in the grey light for love of Thee,
  In mean and darken'd houses:
The scarlet fruits of knowledge and of sin
Have stain'd me with their juice for love of Thee.

I could not choose but sin for love of Thee,
  From Thee so sadly parted;
I could not choose but put away my sin
And purge and scourge those stains for love of Thee.

My soul is sick with life for love of Thee,
  Nothing can ease or fill me:
Restore me, past the frozen baths of death,
My crown and robes, desired for love of Thee:

And take me to Thyself for love of Thee;
  My loss or gain counts little,
But Thou must need me since I need Thee so,
Crying through day and night for love of Thee!

At the End of Things

THE WORLD uprose as a man to find Him—
  Ten thousand methods, ten thousand ends—
Some bent on treasure; the more on pleasure;
  And some on the chaplet which fame attends:
But the great deep's voice in the distance dim
Said: Peace, it is well; they are seeking Him.

When I heard that all the world was questing,
  I look'd for a palmer's staff and found,
By a reed-fringed pond, a fork'd hazel-wand
  On a twisted tree, in a bann'd waste-ground;
But I knew not then what the sounding strings
Of the sea-harps say at the end of things.

They told me, world, you were keen on seeking;
  I cast around for a scrip to hold
Such meagre needs as the roots of weeds—
  All weeds, but one with a root of gold;
Yet I knew not then how the clangs ascend
When the sea-horns peal and the searchings end.

An old worn wallet was that they gave me,
  With twelve old signs on its seven old skins;
And a star I stole for the good of my soul,
  Lest the darkness came down on my sins;
For I knew not who in their life had heard
Of the sea-pipes shrilling a secret word.

I join'd the quest that the world was making,
  Which follow'd the false ways far and wide,
While a thousand cheats in the lanes and streets
  Offer'd that wavering crowd to guide;
But what did they know of the sea-reed's speech
When the peace-words breathe at the end for each?

The fools fell down in the swamps and marshes;
  The fools died hard on the crags and hills;
The lies which cheated, so long repeated,
  Deceived, in spite of their evil wills,
Some knaves themselves at the end of all —
Though how should they hearken when sea-flutes call?

But me the scrip and the staff had strengthen'd;
  I carried the star; that star led me:
The paths I've taken, of most forsaken,
  Do surely lead to an open sea:
As a clamor of voices heard in sleep,
Come shouts through the dark on the shrouded deep.

Now it is noon; in the hush prevailing
  Pipes, harps and horns into flute-notes fall;
The sea, conceding my star's true leading,
  In tongues sublime at the end of all
Gives resonant utterance far and near: —
  'Cast away fear;
  Be of good cheer;
  He is here,
  Is here!'

And now I know that I sought Him only
  Even as child, when for flowers I sought;
In the sins of youth, as in search for truth.
  To find Him, hold Him alone I wrought.
The knaves too seek Him, and fools beguiled —
So speak to them also, sea-voices mild!

Which then was wisdom and which was folly?
  Did my star more than the cozening guide?
The fool, as I think, at the chasm's brink,
  Prone by the swamp or the marsh's side,
Did, even as I, in the end rejoice,
Since the voice of death must be His true voice.

160

A Ladder of Life

FROM age to age in the public place,
  With the under steps in view,
The stairway stands, having earth for base,
  But the heavens it passes through.

  O height and deep,
  And the quests, in sleep,
  Yet the Word of the King says well,
  That the heart of the King is unsearchable.

Of the utmost steps there are legends grand,
  And far stars shine as they roll;
But, of child or man in the wonderful land,
  Is there one who has scaled the whole?

  Yet the great hope stirs,
  Though His thoughts as yours
  Are not, since the first man fell;
  For the heart of the King is unsearchable.

A pulsing song of the stairway strange
  Sing, lark, dissolved in the sky!
But no, for it passes beyond the range
  Of thy song and thy soaring high.

  The star is kin
  To our soul within —
  God orders His world so well:
  Yet the heart of the King is unsearchable.

They say that the angels thereby come down,
  Thereby do the saints ascend,
And that God's light shining from God's own Town
  May be seen at the stairway's end:

For good and ill
May be mixed at will,
The false shew true by a spell,
But the heart of the King is unsearchable.

Now, the stairway stands by the noisy mart
  And the stairway stands by the sea;
About it pulses the world's great heart
  And the heart of yourself and me.

We may read amiss
Both in that and this,
And the truth we read in a well;
Since the heart of the King is unsearchable

For a few steps here and a few steps there
  It is fill'd with our voices loud,
But above these slumbers the silent air
  And the hush of a dreaming cloud.

In the strain and stress
Of that silentness,
Our hearts for the height may swell;
But the heart of the King is unsearchable.

Some few of us, fill'd with a holy fire,
  The Cross and the Christ have kiss'd;
We have sworn to achieve our soul's desire
  By mass and evangelist:

Of step the third
I can bring down word,
And you on the fifth may dwell;
Yet the heart of the King is unsearchable.

As each of us stands at his place assign'd
  And ponders the things we love,
It is meet and right we should call to mind
  That some must have pass'd above:

Yes, some there are
Who have pass'd so far,
They have never return'd to tell;
And the heart of the King is unsearchable.

Some glimpse at least of the end we glean,
  Of the spiral curve and plan;
For stretch as it may through the worlds unseen,
  They are ever the worlds of man;

And — with all spaces —
His mind embraces
The way of the stairs as well —
For his heart, like the King's, is unsearchable.

More Books from Cornerstone

Masonic Enlightenment
The Philosophy, History and Wisdom of Freemasonry
Edited by Michael R. Poll
6x9 Softcover 180 pages
ISBN 1-887560-75-0

God's Soldiers: Roman Catholicism and Freemasonry
by Dudley Wright
6x9 Softcover 96 pages
ISBN 1-887560-71-8

Off in a Dream
A collection of poetry and prose
by Aubrey Damhnait Fae
6x9 Softcover 96 pages
ISBN 1-887560-72-6

A Ghost of a Chance
by Evelyn Klebert
6x9 Softcover 96 pages
ISBN 1-887560-50-5

The Rosicrucians: Their Rites and Mysteries
by Hargrave Jennings
Michael R. Poll, Editor
Large Format, 8.25 x 11 Softcover 276 pages
ISBN 1-887560-88-2

Ancient and Modern Initiation
by Max Heindel
6x9 Softcover 96 pages
ISBN 1-887560-18-1

Cornerstone Book Publishers
www.cornerstonepublishers.com

www.ingramcontent.com/pod-product-compliance
Lightning Source LLC
Chambersburg PA
CBHW021106090426
42738CB00006B/525